PICTURE HISTORY

OF

NEW ENGLAND PASSENGER VESSELS

by

W. BARTLETT CRAM

1980

PUBLISHER: BURNTCOAT CORPORATION
Hampden Highlands, Maine 04445

COPYRIGHT © 1980   BY W. BARTLETT CRAM

LIBRARY OF CONGRESS CARD NUMBER: 80-67991

OTHER PHOTOS

Front jacket and inside front cover:
   Eastern Steamship *BOSTON* coming through the Cape Cod Canal
   in 1924. Courtesy of R. Loren Graham.

Frontispiece:
   BON TON II docked at Brewer Dock (where Chamberlain Bridge
   now stands). The Eastern Boston Steamer *BELFAST* turning at her berth
   at the Bangor Dock. Courtesy of Mildred N. Thayer.

End piece:
   Four steamers at Block Island Dock, left to right:
   PEMAQUID, CAMBRIDGE, WESTPORT and *BLOCK ISLAND*(2)
   (MACHIGONNE). Courtesy of Capt. Raymond H. Abell.

Back jacket and inside back cover:
   Eastern Steamship Line *MASSACHUSETTS* sailing out of Boston
   Harbor en route to New York City. Author's Collection.

PRINTED IN THE UNITED STATES OF AMERICA

First Edition

MAR. — 7 1981

CONTENTS

DEDICATION

TO THE COASTWISE AND COASTAL SEAMEN, WHO LEARNED THEIR PROFESSION ON THE SHIPS PICTURED IN THIS BOOK, AND WHO GAVE THEIR LIVES DURING WORLD WAR I AND WORLD WAR II TO SAVE DEMOCRACY.

PREFACE

PICTURE HISTORY OF NEW ENGLAND PASSENGER VESSELS is an illustrated review of some of the vessels that sailed in the area bounded by Passamaquoddy Bay to the East and Block Island to the West from 1850 to World War II. No mention has been made of the vessels plying Long Island Sound as the subject has been dealt with admirably by Roger Williams McAdam in his books, *The Old Fall River Line, Priscilla of Fall River, Commonwealth Giantess of the Sound,* and *Salts of the Sound.*

Most of the vessels were operating before the advent of automobiles, airplanes and some railroad trains, especially in Maine.

Some of the vessels appear in several chapters, as they were well known in different parts of New England, also, many had several names. Under each picture much of the history of the vessel is given in detail along with statistics.

From babyhood I travelled with my family on the Bangor Line from Boston to Rockland and then on the *J. T. Morse* to Southwest Harbor for the summer. At the end of the season we returned to Greater Boston by the same route. I also was employed for seven summers by the Eastern Steamship Line on many of their vessels.

Therefore, for sentimental reasons, the initial chapters portray the Eastern Steamship Line, Maine Central Railroad Fleet, Swans Island and Vinalhaven Fleet.

ACKNOWLEDGMENT

This picture history required many photographs of the same vessel to present the scene needed to correspond with the history portrayed.

A few photographs were unavailable, as most of the ships were out of existence before this work started. Many hours of research enabled me to accumulate those which are shown.

I am particularly indebted to Reginald R. Clark for his excellent work in reproducing the photographs.

I was able to draw upon the knowledge of Mr. and Mrs. James T. Wilson, John L. Lockhead, W. H. Ballard, C. Bradford Mitchell, and Richard W. Berry, for which I am grateful.

The large number of photographs and the assistance provided by R. Loren Graham, W. H. Ballard, Ernest H. Dickson, Harold W. Castner, Captain Raymond H. Abell, and H. B. Frey, made it possible to produce this book. Without their help it would not have been completed.

Under each picture I have given credit for the photograph and list the names in appreciation.

The Steamship Historical Society of America, Inc.

The Peabody Museum of Salem, Massachusetts

The Mariners Museum, Newport News, Virginia

Deer Isle - Stonington Historical Society (Maine)

The Society for the Preservation of New England Antiquities - Stebbins Collection

Calais Free Library (Maine)

Grand Manan Museum, Grand Manan Island, New Brunswick

The Duke's County Historical Society of Massachusetts

R. Loren Graham, Swampscott, Massachusetts

Captain Raymond H. Abell
W. H. Ballard
R. H. Barbour
J. T. Beck
Michael Bryant
Harold W. Castner
E. E. Claes
R. R. Clark
Sheldon W. Clark
Eng. Ernest H. Dickson
Captain Ross Dickson
Bob Dunton
W. H. Ewen, Jr.
Captain H. G. Foss

W. N. Graffam
Freeman R. Hathaway
Amos W. Kimball
Cecil J. Miller
C. Bradford Mitchell
Sumner T. Pike
Allie Ryan
R. B. Sanborn
A. B. Sides
James Stevens
Chester Swett
Paul D. Tapley
Mildred N. Thayer

ILLUSTRATIONS

MAPS & PLACARD

Chapter I

Eastern Steamship Lines Inc. and Predecessor Companies

Charles Wyman Morse, born in Bath, Maine in 1856, created a number of steamship lines nearly controlling the entire Atlantic coast steamship services at one time.

While attending Bowdoin College, he arranged through several mergers within his family's ice business on the Kennebec and Penobscot Rivers, and their tow boat business, to graduate a very wealthy man. After moving to New York, his position in the financial world allowed him to be successful in the merger of several banks, adding to his wealth.

In 1901 he founded the Eastern Steamship Company by consolidating the Boston & Bangor Steamship Company, Kennebec Steamship Company, Portland Steam Packet Company, International Steamship Company, and Maine Steamship Company. Also, several small companies: Eastern Steamboat Company of Bath, the Rockland, Blue Hill and Ellsworth Steamship Company, and the Portland and Rockland Steamboat Line.

In 1905 he acquired control of the Metropolitan Line (Boston and New York Steamship Service) and merged the Clyde Line, Mallory Line, New York and Cuban Mail Line, and the Hudson Navigation Company into a corporation known as the Consolidated Steamboat Company with Calvin Austin as president.

Mr. Morse put into operation between New York and Boston in 1907, the new *HARVARD* and the *YALE*, which were really ocean liners and very advanced in design. Capable of making twenty-three knots and operating outside of Cape Cod, they left Boston at five o'clock and docked in New York the following morning at eight o'clock. Because passenger capacity was reached on every trip, plans were drawn for two more steamers, the *PRINCETON* and the *DARTMOUTH*.

The Fall River Line, owned by the New Haven Railroad, was given severe competition. The New Haven Railroad magnate, J. P. Morgan and his associates, were so disturbed that a "banker's war" occurred, leaving Mr. Morse in financial embarrassment by being indicted for conspiracy.

J. P. Morgan and the New Haven Railroad actually obtained control of the Consolidated Steamship Company and the *HARVARD* and *YALE*. Later the Federal government required the New Haven to dispose of its interests and the two steamships went to the West Coast.

The Metropolitan Line was merged with the Eastern Steamship Company in 1911. The Clyde Line, Mallory Line and New York and Cuban Mail became the Atlantic, Gulf & West Indies Line.

The Boston and Yarmouth Steamship Company Limited was acquired in 1912. This actually was the marine division of the Dominion Atlantic Railway Company.

The Eastern Steamship Lines was organized in March, 1917. In 1925 the Old Dominion Line, (with service from New York to Norfolk), the Gulf and Southern Steamship Company, and the New York and Richmond Steamship Company were acquired.

The following chapters, IA through IH, contain more details of the Eastern Steamship Lines and their various services.

Chapter IA

Metropolitan Line

Daily passenger and freight service was operated between Boston and New York, with the ships leaving at five o'clock, arriving at the terminus at eight o'clock the next morning.

Passenger service was established in 1906 with the *HARVARD* and the *YALE* operating until 1909. The *BUNKER HILL* and the *MASSACHUSETTS*, originally used by the New Haven Railroad as freighters, were later owned by the Metropolitan Line after extensive passenger accommodations were added to their hulls. These ships ran until World War I.

During the War, the *BELFAST* and *CAMDEN* were used, After the War the *NORTH LAND* and *CALVIN AUSTIN* operated on the Line.

The large, new steamers, *BOSTON* and *NEW YORK*, operated during the summer from 1924 until World War II. The *GEORGE WASHINGTON* and the *ROBERT E. LEE* were used for the winter service.

After the *SAINT JOHN* and *ACADIA* were built they handled the winter Metropolitan Line. Summer and winter services were very popular requiring Eastern to charter the *PRESIDENT WARFIELD* for several summers.

Map Showing
Eastern Steamship Lines
AND CONNECTIONS

3

HARVARD

ROUTE:	Boston - New York Line		NUMBER:	204372
PORTS:	Boston, New York		LENGTH:	376.0
COMPANY:	Metropolitan Steamship Company		BREADTH:	61.3
OTHER NAME:	*CHARLES*		DRAUGHT:	20.2
SISTER SHIP:	*YALE*		GROSS TONNAGE:	3818.0
			SPEED:	23 Knots

BUILT: 1906 - Delaware River I.S.B. & Eng. Wks. Chester, Pennsylvania, December 1.

HISTORY: First trip New York to Boston September 18, 1907.
Final sailing from Boston October 1, 1910.
Spent most of remaining years on San Francisco - San Pedro route.

STATUS: Lost Point Arguello, California, May 30, 1931.

YALE

ROUTE:	Boston - New York Line	NUMBER:	204047
PORTS:	Boston, New York	LENGTH:	376.0
COMPANY:	Metropolitan Steamship Co.	BREADTH:	61.3
OTHER NAME:	*U.S.S. GREYHOUND*	DRAUGHT:	20.2
SISTER SHIP:	*HARVARD*	GROSS TONNAGE:	3818.0
		SPEED:	23 Knots

BUILT: 1907 - Delaware River I.S.B. Eng. Wks. Chester, Pennsylvania, January 30.

HISTORY: July - August 1907, Boston - Saint John Line, three times weekly. First trip Boston - New York,
                   September 18, 1907.
                   Final sailing from Boston, October 2, 1910.

STATUS: Scrapped on West Coast, 1949.

BUNKER HILL

ROUTE:	Boston - New York Line	NUMBER:	204264
PORTS:	Boston, New York	LENGTH:	375.0
COMPANY:	Eastern Steamship Corp.	BREADTH:	52.2
OTHER NAMES:	*U.S.S. AROOSTOOK, S.S. LUX*	DRAUGHT:	16.0
SISTER SHIPS:	*MASSACHUSETTS, OLD COLONY*	GROSS TONNAGE:	4779.0
LOCATION:	Sailing out of Boston, Massachusetts, Harbor	SPEED:	20 Knots
BUILT:	1907 - Wm. Cramp & Sons, Philadelphia, Pennsylvania		

HISTORY: Started as freighter. Rebuilt as passenger ship 1910.
Opened season Boston - New York Line June 25, 1911.
Used Cape Cod Canal June 1, 1916.
Sold to United States Government October 14, 1917. Converted to mine layer.

STATUS: Scrapped on West Coast October 1947.

MASSACHUSETTS

ROUTE: Boston - New York Line
PORTS: Boston, New York
COMPANY: Eastern Steamship Corp.
OTHER NAMES: *U.S.S. SHAWMUT, U.S.S. OGLALA*
SISTER SHIPS: *BUNKER HILL, OLD COLONY*

BUILT: 1907 - Wm. Cramp & Sons, Philadelphia, Pennsylvania.
HISTORY: Started as a freighter. Rebuilt as a passenger ship in 1910.
Opened season Boston - New York Line June 25, 1911.
Used on Cape Cod Canal June 1, 1916.
Sold to United State Government, October 14, 1917. Converted to mine layer. Attacked at Pearl Harbor, reconditioned, served in World War II successfully as Tender.
STATUS: Sold by War Shipping Administration March 1947. Abandoned 1972.

NUMBER: 204012
LENGTH: 375.0
BREADTH: 52.2
DRAUGHT: 16.0
GROSS TONNAGE: 4779.0
SPEED: 20 Knots

BOSTON (2)

ROUTE:	Boston - New York Line		NUMBER:	223749
PORTS:	Boston, New York		LENGTH:	385.3
COMPANY:	Eastern Steamship Lines Inc.		BREADTH:	72.5
OTHER NAMES:	*S.S. BOSTON* (British)		DRAUGHT:	20.9
SISTER SHIP:	*NEW YORK* (2)		GROSS TONNAGE:	4989.0
			SPEED:	19 Knots

BUILT: 1924 - Bethlehem Steel Co., Sparrows Point, Maryland.

HISTORY: June 4, 1924, sailed Boston to New York.
November 28, 1941, final trip from New York to Boston.
December 29, 1941, sold to United States Government and turned over to British Ministry of Shipping.

STATUS: Sunk September 26, 1942, by U-Boat.

R. Loren Graham

NEW YORK (2)

ROUTE:	Boston - New York Line		NUMBER:	223901
PORTS:	Boston, New York		LENGTH:	385.3
COMPANY:	Eastern Steamship Lines Inc.		BREADTH:	72.5
OTHER NAMES:	*S.S. NEW YORK* (British)		DRAUGHT:	20.9
SISTER SHIP:	*BOSTON* (2)		GROSS TONNAGE:	4989.0
			SPEED:	19 Knots

BUILT: 1924 - Bethlehem Steel Co., Sparrows Point, Maryland.

HISTORY: July 4, 1924, sailed Boston to New York.
            November 29, 1941, final trip from New York to Boston.
            December 29, 1941, sold to United States Government and turned over to British Ministry of Shipping.

STATUS: Sunk September 25, 1942, by U-Boat.

GEORGE WASHINGTON

ROUTE:	Winter, Boston - New York Line	NUMBER:	224216
PORTS:	Boston, New York	LENGTH:	375.5
COMPANY:	Eastern Steamship Lines Inc.	BREADTH:	54.0
OTHER NAME:	*S.S. GASCOGNE* (France)	DRAUGHT:	17.2
SISTER SHIP:	*ROBERT E. LEE*	GROSS TONNAGE:	5184.0
		SPEED:	15 Knots

BUILT: 1924 - Newport News, Virginia, S.B. & D.D. Co.

HISTORY: About December 1, 1927, entered Winter service Boston - New York Line.
Last trip Boston - New York Line, April 18, 1932.
Operated Summers New York - Norfolk Line.
Year round New York - Norfolk Line after April, 1932.
During World War II, used as United States Army Transport.
Sold to French Line 1949.

STATUS: Sold to Chinese shipbreakers 1955.

R. Loren Graham

ROBERT E. LEE

ROUTE:	Winter, Boston - New York Line	NUMBER:	224339
PORTS:	Boston, New York	LENGTH:	375.5
COMPANY:	Eastern Steamship Lines Inc.	BREADTH:	54.0
SISTER SHIP:	*GEORGE WASHINGTON*	DRAUGHT:	17.2
LOCATION:	Sailing in East River, New York City.	GROSS TONNAGE:	5184.0
BUILT:	1924 - Newport News, Virginia, S.B. & D.D. Co.	SPEED:	15 Knots

HISTORY: November 7, 1927, inaugurated Winter service Boston - New York Line.
Last trip April 18, 1932, Boston - New York Line.
Operated Summers New York - Norfolk Line until War.
Year round New York - Norfolk Line after April, 1932.
During World War II used as United States Army Transport.

STATUS: Sunk July 30, 1942, by Nazi Submarine in Gulf of Mexico, eighty miles below New Orleans, Louisiana.

11

PRESIDENT WARFIELD

ROUTE:	Chartered Summer 1930 - Used as second section three nights a week on Boston - New York Line.	NUMBER:	227753
		LENGTH:	320.0
PORTS:	Boston, New York	BREADTH:	56.6
COMPANY:	Old Bay Line, owner:	DRAUGHT:	16.9
	Eastern Steamship Lines Inc., Charterer.	GROSS TONNAGE:	1814.0
OTHER NAMES:	*RUTH GRUBER, EXODUS 1947*		
BUILT:	1928 - Pusey & Jones Co., Wilmington, Delaware.		
HISTORY:	Ran most of life on Chesapeake Bay Run.		

HISTORY: Ran most of life on Chesapeake Bay Run.
Converted to War Transport and operated by British Ministry of War Transport during World War II.
Purchased by the Haganah and ran blockade into Palestine.

STATUS: Dismantled in Haifa, Israel, March, 1953.

SAINT JOHN

ROUTE:	Winter, Boston - New York	NUMBER:	231530
	Summer, Boston - Saint John, New Brunswick	LENGTH:	387.4
PORTS:	Boston, New York, Boston, Saint John	BREADTH:	61.2
COMPANY:	Eastern Steamship Lines, Inc.	DRAUGHT:	22.6
OTHER NAMES:	U.S.S. RESCUE, U.S.S. ANTAEUS	GROSS TONNAGE:	6185.0
SISTER SHIP:	ACADIA	SPEED:	18 Knots
LOCATION:	Off Newport News, Virginia		

BUILT: 1932 - Newport News, Virginia, S.B. & D.D. Co.

HISTORY: May 2, 1932, first trip Boston - Saint John, New Brunswick.
November 1, 1932, first trip Boston - New York Line.
In 1939, ran New York - Yarmouth, Nova Scotia - Boston.
In 1940, ran New York - Portland - Bar Harbor, one round trip a week; New York - Yarmouth, one round trip a week.
March 16, 1941, final trip New York - Boston.
During World War II operated as Submarine Tender, Transport, and Hospital Ship.
In 1946 sold by War Shipping Administration from Olympia Layup Fleet.

STATUS: Burned at Seattle, Washington, January 31, 1959. Louis Schwartz, owner of the Railway Terminal, was in the process of scrapping the ship.

ACADIA

ROUTE:	Winter, Boston - New York	NUMBER:	231673
	Summer, New York - Portland - Bar Harbor	LENGTH:	387.4
PORTS:	Boston, New York, Portland, Bar Harbor	BREADTH:	61.2
COMPANY:	Eastern Steamship Lines, Inc.	DRAUGHT:	22.6
SISTER SHIP:	SAINT JOHN	GROSS TONNAGE:	6185.0
LOCATION:	Off Newport News, Virginia	SPEED:	18 Knots
BUILT:	1932 - Newport News, Virginia, S.B. & D.D. Co.		

HISTORY: New York - Yarmouth, Summer service, 1932.
October 5, 1932, first trip Boston - New York Line, New York - Portland, Summer Service 1939, and also New York - Bermuda.
March 17, 1941, final trip, New York - Boston.
During World War II operated as Transport and Hospital Ship.

STATUS: September, 1955, sold to Swiss operated company.

Chapter IB

Maine Steamship Line

This was one of the most lucrative lines on the Atlantic seaboard.

Service was established in 1890 with two new wooden steamers, *COTTAGE CITY* and *MANHATTAN*, operating several times a week between Portland and New York. During the first few years a stop was made en route at Martha's Vineyard.

These were followed by the steel ships, *JOHN ENGLIS*, *HORATIO HALL*, and *NORTH STAR*. The first was sold, the second lost in a fire, the remaining, *NORTH STAR*, ran with the new *NORTH LAND*.

The Eastern Steamship Lines received the former New Haven steamer, *OLD COLONY*, which provided excellent service after passenger accommodations were added.

Following World War I the *CALVIN AUSTIN* operated on the route, followed by the new *FLORIDA*, which was chartered from the Peninsular & Occidental Steamship Company. She was later replaced by the new, large, Clyde liner *IROQUOIS*.

The last vessel to operate on the line was the steamship *SAINT JOHN*.

Society for the Preservation of New England Antiquities

COTTAGE CITY

ROUTE: Portland - New York
PORTS: Portland, Oak Bluffs, New York
COMPANY: Maine Steamship Co.
SISTER SHIP: *MANHATTAN*
LOCATION: Portland Harbor, Maine

NUMBER: 126613
LENGTH: 233.2
BREADTH: 40.1
DRAUGHT: 24.1
GROSS TONNAGE: 1892.0

BUILT: 1890 - New England Shipbuilding Co., Bath, Maine.
HISTORY: Brought to the West Coast in 1899 for the Seattle - Skagway Gold Rush Trade.
STATUS: Wrecked at Cape Mudge, British Columbia, January 26, 1911. Total loss.
Struck rocks, thirty-seven passengers and crew of sixty landed safely.

MANHATTAN

ROUTE:	Portland - New York	NUMBER	92280
PORTS:	Portland, Oak Bluffs, New York	LENGTH:	233.2
COMPANY:	Maine Steamship Co.	BREADTH:	40.1
SISTER SHIP:	*COTTAGE CITY*	DRAUGHT:	25.1
		GROSS TONNAGE:	1892.0

BUILT: 1890 - New England Shipbuilding Co., Bath, Maine.
HISTORY: On the Portland - New York Line entire life.
STATUS: Cotton cargo caught fire at a Portland wharf March 7, 1910. Ship total loss.

JOHN ENGLIS

ROUTE:	Portland - New York	NUMBER:	77240
PORTS:	Portland, New York	LENGTH:	297.0
COMPANY:	Maine Steamship Co.	BREADTH:	46.0
OTHER NAMES:	*U.S.S. RELIEF, U.S.S. REPOSE*	DRAUGHT:	17.0
SISTER SHIPS:	*HORATIO HALL, NORTH STAR*	GROSS TONNAGE:	3168.0
		SPEED:	16 Knots

BUILT: 1898 - Delaware River Co., Chester, Pennsylvania.

HISTORY: Sold May 20, 1898, to United States Government for Hospital ship in Spanish-American War. Sold by Navy, January 9, 1922. Renamed *HAINING, MINDANAO, LANAO.*

HORATIO HALL

ROUTE: Portland - New York
PORTS: Portland, New York
COMPANY: Maine Steamship Co.
SISTER SHIPS: *JOHN ENGLIS, NORTH STAR*

NUMBER: 96401
LENGTH: 297.0
BREADTH: 46.0
DRAUGHT: 17.0
GROSS TONNAGE: 3168.0
SPEED: 16 Knots

BUILT: 1898 - Delaware River Co., Chester, Pennsylvania.
HISTORY: Ran entire life on the Portland - New York Line.
STATUS: Sunk by collision with Metropolitan Line freighter, *H. F. DIMOCK*, March 10, 1909, in dense fog in
                Pollock's Rip Slue.
                Abandoned by underwriters and removed by explosion.

NORTH STAR

ROUTE:	Portland - New York	NUMBER:	130924
PORTS:	Portland, New York	LENGTH:	298.8
COMPANY:	Maine Steamship Company	BREADTH:	46.0
	Eastern Steamship Company	DRAUGHT:	17.2
SISTER SHIPS:	*JOHN ENGLIS, HORATIO HALL*	GROSS TONNAGE:	3159.0
		SPEED:	16 Knots

BUILT: 1901 - Chester, Pennsylvania.

HISTORY: Ran several years from Portland - New York; also a number of years from Boston - Yarmouth, Nova Scotia, on the Boston - Yarmouth Line.

STATUS: Stranded on Green Island Ledge, Nova Scotia, August 8, 1919. 348 on board, no lives lost. August 9, 1919, condemned.

NORTH LAND

ROUTE:	Portland - New York		NUMBER:	207282
PORTS:	Portland, New York		LENGTH:	304.4
COMPANY:	Maine Steamship Co.		BREADTH:	47.2
	Eastern Steamship Lines, Inc.		DRAUGHT:	15.6
			GROSS TONNAGE:	3121.0
			SPEED:	17 Knots

BUILT: 1910 - Harlan & Hollingsworth Co., Wilmington, Delaware.

HISTORY: Built for Portland - New York Line. Used on Boston - New York Line for five years. Used also on Boston - Yarmouth Line. Chartered to Peninsular & Occidental Company for Winter of 1923 and several other Winters.

STATUS: Scrapped 1934, Baltimore, Maryland.

OLD COLONY

ROUTE:	Portland - New York	NUMBER:	204528
PORTS:	Portland, New York	LENGTH:	375.0
COMPANY:	Eastern Steamship Corp.	BREADTH:	52.2
SISTER SHIPS:	*BUNKER HILL, MASSACHUSETTS*	DRAUGHT:	16.0
LOCATION:	An East River Dock in New York City	GROSS TONNAGE:	4779.0
	near Brooklyn Bridge.	SPEED:	20 Knots

BUILT: 1907 - Wm. Cramp & Sons, Philadelphia, Pennsylvania.

HISTORY: Sold November 17, 1917, to United States Navy Department.
Then turned over to British Government.

STATUS: Scrapped in Germany, September, 1922. Had bad boilers.

FLORIDA

ROUTE:	Portland - New York	NUMBER:	230773
PORTS:	New York, Portland, Bar Harbor	LENGTH:	365.0
COMPANY:	Peninsular & Occidental Steamship Co., Owner.	BREADTH:	56.6
	Eastern Steamship Lines, Charterer.	DRAUGHT:	28.6
LOCATION:	Sailing out of Portland Harbor	GROSS TONNAGE:	2689.0
		SPEED:	19½ Knots

BUILT: 1931 - Newport News, Virginia, S.B. & D.D. Co.

HISTORY: Chartered for Summers, 1934-35.
Transferred to Liberian Flag, 1956.
November 14, 1957, transferred from Havana Run to Miami - Nassau Service.

IROQUOIS

ROUTE:	Portland - New York - Bar Harbor	NUMBER:	226332
PORTS:	New York, Portland, Bar Harbor	LENGTH:	409.6
COMPANY:	Clyde Steamship Co., Owner.	BREADTH:	62.2
	Eastern Steamship Lines, Charterer.	DRAUGHT:	19.4
OTHER NAMES:	*U.S.S. SOLACE, ANKARA*	GROSS TONNAGE:	6210.0
SISTER SHIP:	*SHAWNEE*	SPEED:	17 Knots
LOCATION:	Sailing out of East River, New York, to Maine		
BUILT:	1927 - Newport News, Virginia, S.B. & D.D. Co.		

HISTORY: Ran Summer 1936. First trip June 26. Built for Clyde Line's New York - Miami Trade. Sold to
United States Navy July 19, 1940, for use as Hospital Ship.

STATUS: As of 1961, on Istanbul, Piraeus, Naples, Genoa, Marseilles Run.

Chapter ICa

Boston - Yarmouth Line

The Canadian steamers, YARMOUTH and BOSTON were used for a number of years, being replaced by PRINCE EDWARD and later by PRINCE ARTHUR and PRINCE GEORGE. These two ships were requisitioned by the British Admiralty for World War I. The American NORTH STAR replaced them during this period. After the War PRINCE ARTHUR and PRINCE GEORGE returned to the line for a few years, later replaced by the NORTH LAND. In 1926 two beautiful new liners, YARMOUTH (2) and EVANGELINE (2), were operated under the American flag as the Yarmouth line.

Chapter ICb

New York - Yarmouth Line

This service was established in 1926 with the EVANGELINE (2). After the ACADIA was built she serviced not only Yarmouth but went on to Saint John, New Brunswick. The EVANGELINE (2) eventually joined the YARMOUTH (2) providing daily service from Boston to Yarmouth, Nova Scotia.

YARMOUTH (Canadian)

ROUTE: Yarmouth - Boston
PORTS: Yarmouth, Boston
COMPANY: Yarmouth Steamship Co.
OTHER NAME: *FREDERICK DOUGLASS*

NUMBER: 93373
LENGTH: 220.3
BREADTH: 35.0
DRAUGHT: 12.7
GROSS TONNAGE: 1452.0
SPEED: 14 Knots

BUILT: 1887 - A. McMillan & Son, Dunbarton, Scotland.
HISTORY: First trip between Boston and Yarmouth May 8, 1887.
STATUS: Scrapped 1925.

BOSTON (Canadian)

ROUTE: Yarmouth - Boston
PORTS: Yarmouth, Boston
COMPANY: Yarmouth Steamship Co.
Eastern Steamship Corp.
OTHER NAME: *U.S.S. CAMBRIDGE*
BUILT: 1890 - A. Stephen & Son Ltd., Glasgow, Scotland.
HISTORY: Sold June, 1917, to United States Navy.
STATUS: Scrapped 1922.

NUMBER: 98585
LENGTH: 245.0
BREADTH: 36.0
DRAUGHT: 20.0
GROSS TONNAGE: 1694.0

PRINCE EDWARD (Canadian)

ROUTE:	Yarmouth - Boston	NUMBER:	106037
PORTS:	Yarmouth, Boston	LENGTH:	268.0
COMPANY:	Dominion Atlantic Railway Co.	BREADTH:	33.2
OTHER NAMES:	(Dan) *PRINS GUSTAF ADOLPH*	DRAUGHT:	12.4
	(Russian) *VASILIJ VELIKIJ*	GROSS TONNAGE:	1414.0
BUILT:	1897 - Earle Shipbuilding Co., Hull, England.		
HISTORY:	Operated several years on Boston - Yarmouth Line. Sold to German parties and later Russian.		
STATUS:	Wrecked March 3, 1916, on voyage to Vardar, Russia.		

PRINCE ARTHUR (Canadian)

ROUTE:	Yarmouth - Boston	NUMBER:	40131
PORTS:	Yarmouth, Boston	LENGTH:	290.0
COMPANY:	Boston & Yarmouth Steamship Co., Ltd.	BREADTH:	38.0
	Eastern Steamship Corp.	DRAUGHT:	16.5
SISTER SHIP:	PRINCE GEORGE	GROSS TONNAGE:	2040.0
		SPEED:	20 Knots

BUILT: 1899 - Earle Co., Hull, England.

HISTORY: Bought by Eastern Steamship Corp. 1912.
Used by British Admiralty during World War I as Hospital Ship.

STATUS: Broken up 1929.

PRINCE GEORGE (Canadian)

ROUTE:	Yarmouth - Boston	NUMBER:	110003
PORTS:	Yarmouth, Boston	LENGTH:	290.0
COMPANY:	Boston & Yarmouth Steamship Co., Ltd.	BREADTH:	38.0
	Eastern Steamship Corp.	DRAUGHT:	16.5
SISTER SHIP:	*PRINCE ARTHUR*	GROSS TONNAGE:	2040.0
LOCATION:	Sailing out of Boston Harbor, Massachusetts	SPEED:	20 Knots
BUILT:	1899 - Earle Co., Hull, England.		
HISTORY:	Bought by Eastern Steamship Corp. 1912.		
	Used by British Admiralty as Hospital Ship during World War I,		
STATUS:	Broken up 1931.		

YARMOUTH (2)

ROUTE:	Boston - Yarmouth Line	NUMBER:	226635
PORTS:	Boston, Yarmouth	LENGTH:	378.0
COMPANY:	Eastern Steamship Lines, Inc.	BREADTH:	55.6
OTHER NAMES:	*YARMOUTH CASTLE, QUEEN OF NASSAU*	DRAUGHT:	21.3
	YARMOUTH CASTLE, YARMOUTH	GROSS TONNAGE:	5043.0
SISTER SHIP:	*EVANGELINE*	SPEED:	16.5 Knots

BUILT: 1927 - Wm. Cramp & Sons Ship & Engine Co., Philadelphia, Pennsylvania.

HISTORY: Maiden voyage Boston - Yarmouth, July 9, 1927. Made several Winter cruises from Boston and New York to the West Indies. In 1939 made trips to Saint John, New Brunswick, and Digby, Nova Scotia, in addition to Boston and Yarmouth Service.
Used as a United States Army Transport during World War II.

STATUS: Operating out of Miami, 1966.

31

EVANGELINE (2)

ROUTE:	Boston - Yarmouth Line		NUMBER:	226690
PORTS:	Boston, Yarmouth		LENGTH:	378.0
COMPANY:	Eastern Steamship Lines Inc.		BREADTH:	55.6
OTHER NAME:	*YARMOUTH CASTLE*		DRAUGHT:	21.3
SISTER SHIP:	*YARMOUTH*		GROSS TONNAGE:	5043.0
			SPEED:	16.5 Knots

BUILT: 1927 - Wm. Cramp & Sons Ship & Engine Co., Philadelphia, Pennsylvania.

HISTORY: Used as a United States Army Transport during World War II.
Sold November 7, 1954.
Transferred to Liberian Flag, 1955.
Arrived in New York late June, 1964, as *YARMOUTH CASTLE*.

STATUS: Sunk November 13, 1965.

Chapter ID

International Line

This line was originally established for service from Boston to Eastport, Lubec and Saint John, using the paddle-wheel steamers: *NEW YORK, NEW BRUNSWICK,* and *NEW ENGLAND.*

The *NEW YORK* was sold and replaced by the *FALMOUTH.* Later the service continued with the steamers *STATE OF MAINE* and *CUMBERLAND.* Part of one year the Clyde Line's *HURON* was chartered. Following this the wooden, propellor-driven *ST. CROIX* was built and shortly after, service was provided by *GOVERNOR DINGLEY, CALVIN AUSTIN,* and *GOVERNOR COBB.* The following steamers made several trips: *CAMDEN, YALE,* Canadian *PRINCE ARTHUR,* and *RANSOM B. FULLER.*

After the Yarmouth Line had its new ships, the *NORTH LAND* operated on the International Line for several years. The beautiful, new *SAINT JOHN* replaced the *NORTH LAND* running from Boston to Saint John, New Brunswick.

NEW YORK

ROUTE: Boston - Portland - Saint John, New Brunswick

PORTS: Boston, Portland, Lubec, Eastport, Saint John, New Brunswick

COMPANY: International Steamship Co.

LOCATION: At Eastport, Maine

BUILT: 1852 - Clayton, New York.

HISTORY: Remained on International Line until 1885.
During Civil War, used to exchange prisoners on the James River, Virginia.

STATUS: Burned at head of North Fifth Street, Camden, New Jersey, May 31, 1894.

NUMBER: 18324

LENGTH: 223.1

BREADTH: 33.4

DRAUGHT: 12.0

GROSS TONNAGE: 1110.0

NEW BRUNSWICK

ROUTE:	Boston - New Brunswick		NUMBER:	18322
PORTS:	Boston, Portland, Lubec, Eastport,		LENGTH:	220.4
	Saint John, New Brunswick		BREADTH:	31.0
COMPANY:	International Steamship Co.		DRAUGHT:	18.7
LOCATION:	At Eastport, Maine		GROSS TONNAGE:	935.28
BUILT:	1860 - J. Englis, New York, New York.			

HISTORY: Operated Boston - Bangor Line after loss of Steamship *CAMBRIDGE*. 1898 operated for the Colonial Steamboat Co., New London, Connecticut. Later operated as Excursion Steamer around Boston.

STATUS: Abandoned 1906.

NEW ENGLAND

ROUTE:	Boston - Saint John, New Brunswick		NUMBER:	18323
PORTS:	Boston, Portland, Eastport, Lubec,		LENGTH:	240.0
	Saint John, New Brunswick		BREADTH:	32.0
COMPANY:	International Steamship Co.		DRAUGHT:	14.9
OTHER NAME:	CITY OF PORTLAND (not to be confused		GROSS TONNAGE:	1025.78
	with the PORTLAND)			
LOCATION:	Portland, Maine			
BUILT:	1862 - John Englis Co., New York, New York			
HISTORY:	Struck "Wolves" Ledge near Eastport, Maine, in dense fog July 22, 1872, partly filled. Raised and rebuilt as CITY OF PORTLAND May, 1884.			
STATUS:	Ran ashore near Rockland, Maine. Became total loss.			
NOTE:	Unable to find picture as NEW ENGLAND.			

FALMOUTH

ROUTE:	Boston - Saint John, New Brunswick	NUMBER:	120019
PORTS:	Boston, Portland, Lubec, Eastport,	LENGTH:	232.1
	Saint John, New Brunswick	BREADTH:	36.4
COMPANY:	International Steamship Co.	DRAUGHT:	14.2
LOCATION:	At Commercial Wharf in Boston, Massachusetts	GROSS TONNAGE:	1156.0
BUILT:	1872 - New York, New York.		
HISTORY:	Ran entire life on International Line.		
STATUS:	While undergoing repairs at Portland, Maine, caught fire and was totally destroyed April 29, 1884.		

STATE OF MAINE

ROUTE: International Line
PORTS: Boston, Portland, Lubec, Eastport,
                Saint John, New Brunswick
COMPANY: International Steamship Co.
OTHER NAMES: *EDGEMONT, CAPE MAY*
BUILT: 1882 - New England Steamship Co., Bath, Maine.
HISTORY: Sold 1902 to Joy Line.
STATUS: Burned September 24, 1925, for old metal.

NUMBER: 115856
LENGTH: 241.0
BREADTH: 37.1
DRAUGHT: 14.6
GROSS TONNAGE: 1409.0

CUMBERLAND

ROUTE: International Line
PORTS: Boston, Portland, Lubec, Eastport,
Saint John, New Brunswick
COMPANY: International Steamship Co.
OTHER NAME: *LARCHMONT*
BUILT: 1885 - New England Shipbuilding Co., Bath, Maine.
HISTORY: Sold 1902 to Joy Line.
STATUS: Lost in collision, February 11, 1907.

NUMBER: 126281
LENGTH: 252.2
BREADTH: 37.0
DRAUGHT: 14.8
GROSS TONNAGE: 1606.0

ST. CROIX

ROUTE: International Line

PORTS: Boston, Portland, Lubec, Eastport,
Saint John, New Brunswick

COMPANY: International Steamship Co.
Eastern Steamship Co.

BUILT: August 8, 1895 - New England Shipbuilding Co., Bath, Maine.

HISTORY: Sold in Boston, November 7, 1906, to the Enterprise Transportation Co. Taken to West Coast for trade with Nome, Alaska, 1909.

STATUS: Destroyed by fire near Santa Monica, California, November 11, 1911. One hundred sixty-nine on board, no lives lost.

NUMBER: 116698
LENGTH: 240.7
BREADTH: 40.4
DRAUGHT: 25.9
GROSS TONNAGE: 1994.0

HURON

ROUTE:	International Line	NUMBER:	96658
PORTS:	Boston, Lubec, Eastport	LENGTH:	291.2
COMPANY:	Clyde Steamship Co., Owner.	BREADTH:	43.1
	Eastern Steamship Co., Charterer,	DRAUGHT:	20.6
SISTER SHIP:	*KIOWA*	GROSS TONNAGE:	3318.0
		SPEED:	12 Knots

BUILT: 1902 - Wm. Cramp & Sons Co., Philadelphia, Pennsylvania.

HISTORY: Chartered to Eastern Steamship Co., Summer of 1906.
           Ran for many years on the Clyde Steamship Company's Boston - Jacksonville Line.

STATUS: Abandoned June 30, 1932.

GOVERNOR DINGLEY

ROUTE:	International Line	NUMBER:	86483
PORTS:	Boston, Lubec, Eastport,	LENGTH:	298.6
	Saint John, New Brunswick	BREADTH:	60.8
COMPANY:	Portland Steam Packet Co.	DRAUGHT:	17.8
	Eastern Steamship Lines Inc.	GROSS TONNAGE:	3826.0
LOCATION:	Boston Harbor, Massachusetts	SPEED:	16 Knots

BUILT: 1898 - Delaware River Iron & Shipbuilding Co., Chester, Pennsylvania, September 5, 1898.

HISTORY: Built to replace lost steamer *PORTLAND*.
First trip December 10, 1899, Boston - Portland.
International Line, 1908 to 1918.
United States Shipping Board, 1919, as Training Ship.
International Line, 1920 to September 6, 1932.

STATUS: In 1934 wreckers started their work at Baltimore, Maryland.

CALVIN AUSTIN

ROUTE:	International Line	NUMBER:	127768
PORTS:	Boston, Lubec, Eastport,	LENGTH:	298.1
	Saint John, New Brunswick	BREADTH:	60.8
COMPANY:	Eastern Steamship Lines Inc.	DRAUGHT:	17.8
LOCATION:	Boston Harbor, Massachusetts	GROSS TONNAGE:	3826.0
		SPEED:	16 Knots

BUILT: 1903 - Delaware River Iron & Shipbuilding Co., Chester, Pennsylvania.

HISTORY: Operated on International Line prior to World War I.
United States Shipping Board Training Ship, World War I.
After World War I, ran until 1925 on Boston - New York Line.
1926, ran from New York to Portland. Later Portland to Boston.

STATUS: Sold July 3, 1934, to Boston Iron & Metal Co., Baltimore, Maryland, for wrecking.

The Deer Isle - Stonington Historical Society

GOVERNOR COBB

ROUTE:	International Line	NUMBER:	203584
PORTS:	Boston, Lubec, Eastport,	LENGTH:	289.1
	Saint John, New Brunswick	BREADTH:	54.0
COMPANY:	Eastern Steamship Lines Inc.	DRAUGHT:	18.0
OTHER NAME:	*U.S.S. COBB*	GROSS TONNAGE:	2522.0
		SPEED:	18 Knots
		(19.2 on Maiden Trip)	

BUILT: 1906 - Delaware River Iron & Shipbuilding Company, Chester, Pennsylvania.

HISTORY: First Turbine Propelled Commercial Ship in the United States.
Chartered several Winters to Peninsular & Occidental Steamship Co. A United States Shipping Board Training Ship during World War I. Sold to Peninsular & Occidental Company in 1920. During World War II used as United States Coast Guard Combat Ship. During Normandy invasion served as a Helicopter Mother Ship.

STATUS: Broken up 1948.

Chapter IE

Bangor Line

This service was established in 1882 as the Boston & Bangor Steamship Company, becoming part of the Eastern Steamship Line in 1901. At first *KATAHDIN* and *CAMBRIDGE* were used and later *FOREST CITY* and *LEWISTON*.

The new steamer *PENOBSCOT* operated on this Line, followed by the *CITY OF BANGOR* and the *CITY OF ROCKLAND*. *JOHN BROOKS* and *RANSOM B. FULLER* made several trips during this period. These vessels were all paddle-wheel steamers.

The ships, *CAMDEN* and *BELFAST* operated respectively, from 1907 and 1909, for many years. The *GOVERNOR COBB* was withdrawn, after her initial trip proved she was unsuitable for the route. Assisting with the large cargoes designated for the *CAMDEN* and *BELFAST* were the freighters, *BENEFACTOR* and *CORNISH*.

Having single hulls, *CAMDEN* and *BELFAST* were not able to continue on the Bangor Line after the *MORRO CASTLE* disaster. New safety legislation was enacted by Congress affecting ships of this type.

The Bangor Line's last trip was made on December 28, 1935.

BOSTON AND BANGOR

ELEGANT STEAMERS

COOL OCEAN BREEZES

BEAUTIFUL SCENERY

A FULL NIGHT'S REST

THE SANFORD STEAMSHIP COMPANY

1881 | FALL ARRANGEMENT | 1881

4 TRIPS PER WEEK 4

STEAMER	STEAMER
KATAHDIN	**CAMBRIDGE**

COMMENCING SEPT. 19, 1881, UNTIL FURTHER NOTICE

WILL LEAVE LINCOLN'S WHARF, FOOT OF BATTERY ST., BOSTON, FOR BANGOR,

Every MONDAY, TUESDAY, THURSDAY and FRIDAY, at **5.00** P.M., touching at ROCKLAND, CAMDEN, BELFAST, SEARSPORT, BUCKSPORT, WINTERPORT, and HAMPDEN. RETURNING, one of the above Steamers will leave BANGOR for BOSTON every MONDAY, WEDNESDAY, THURSDAY, and SATURDAY, at **11.00** A.M., touching as above.

CONNECTIONS made at Rockland with K. & L. R.R. for Thomaston. Warren, Waldoboro', Damariscotta and other stations; with steamers for SOUTHWEST and BAR HARBOR every TUESDAY, WEDNESDAY and SATURDAY MORNING; for Lamoine, Ellsworth, Hancock and Sullivan every TUESDAY and SATURDAY MORNING; for Castine, Deer Isle, Sedgwick, Millbridge, Jonesport and Machiasport, every WEDNESDAY and SATURDAY MORNING; for Northwest Harbor, Deer Isle, Blue Hill and Ellsworth, every WEDNESDAY and SATURDAY MORNING. **RETURNING**— Passengers from Mt. Desert connect at Rockland every MONDAY, WEDNESDAY and THURSDAY EVENING with steamer for Boston direct; from Machiasport, Millbridge, etc., connect at Rockland every MONDAY and THURSDAY EVENING; from Sullivan, Lamoine, etc., connect at Rockland every MONDAY and WEDNESDAY EVENING; from Ellsworth, Blue Hill, Northwest Harbor and Deer Isle, MONDAY and THURSDAY EVENING; arriving in Boston the following morning. At Belfast with steamers for and from Castine, Islesboro and Brooksville.

Also for all stations on Belfast & M. L. R.R.; at Bucksport with stage for and from Bluehill and Ellsworth, four times per week each way; at Bangor for MOOSEHEAD LAKE and all stations on E. & N. A. R.R. and B. & P. R.R.

GOING WEST.—TICKETS sold on each steamer for Lowell, Lawrence, New York, Philadelphia, Baltimore and Washington, and Baggage Checked Through if desired. Also Tickets for the West and Southwest, via Pennsylvania Central, Lake Shore and Great Western Railroads.

FOR PORTLAND.—The steamer of this Line leaving Bangor on MONDAY and THURSDAY connects at Rockland with steamer for Portland direct. Passengers from Bangor and River Landings ticketed through.

EXCURSION TICKETS

SOLD BY THIS LINE AT THE FOLLOWING RATES:

Boston to ROCKLAND and Return - - $4.00	Boston to BUCKSPORT and Return - - $5.75
" CAMDEN and Return - - 4.25	" WINTERPORT and Return - 5.85
" BELFAST and Return - - 5.00	" BANGOR and Return - - - 6.00
" SEARSPORT and Return - 5.25	

EXCURSION TICKETS *from these places to BOSTON AND RETURN at same rates.*
STATEROOMS *may be obtained by communicating with the Agent at the place from which passage is to be taken.*

AGENTS O. A. KALLOCH, Rockland; E. M. WOOD, Camden; DANIEL LANE, Belfast; JOSEPH FIELD, Searsport; J. W. PATTERSON, Bucksport; JOHN STOKELL, Winterport; GEO. A. DELANO, Hampden; S. G. DOWNES, Bangor.

W. H. HILL, Jr., Treasurer. **JAMES LITTLEFIELD, Sup't.**

9-9-81. Rand, Avery & Co., Printers, Boston.

KATAHDIN

ROUTE:	Boston - Bangor Line	NUMBER:	14028
PORTS:	Boston, Rockland, Camden, Northport,	LENGTH:	241.0
	Belfast, Searsport, Bucksport, Winterport,	BREADTH:	35.0
	Hampden, Bangor.	DRAUGHT:	11.6
COMPANY:	Sanford Steamship Co.	GROSS TONNAGE:	1234.0
LOCATION:	Winterport, Maine, Dock		
BUILT:	1863 - John Englis & Son, New York, New York.		
HISTORY:	Winter, 1864, chartered by Fall River Line.		
STATUS:	1895 dismantled at Nut Island, Quincy, Massachusetts.		

CAMBRIDGE

ROUTE:	Boston - Bangor Line	NUMBER:	5502
PORTS:	Boston, Rockland, Camden, Northport,	LENGTH:	250.0
	Belfast, Searsport, Bucksport, Winterport	BREADTH:	38.0
	Hampden, Bangor.	DRAUGHT:	12.0
COMPANY:	Sanford Steamship Co.	GROSS TONNAGE:	1337.0
LOCATION:	Foster's Wharf, Boston, Massachusetts		
BUILT:	1867 - John Englis & Sons, New York, New York.		
HISTORY:	Only Boston-Bangor steamer lost in more than one hundred years of operation.		
STATUS:	Struck Old Man's Ledge off Port Clyde, Maine, February 10, 1886. Broke in two under strain of heavy seas. All passengers and crew saved.		

PENOBSCOT

ROUTE:	Boston - Bangor Line	NUMBER:	150253
PORTS:	Boston, Rockland, Camden, Northport,	LENGTH:	255.0
	Belfast, Searsport, Bucksport, Winterport,	BREADTH:	38.0
	Hampden, Bangor.	DRAUGHT:	13.0
COMPANY:	Boston & Bangor Steamship Co.	GROSS TONNAGE:	1414.0
LOCATION:	On Penobscot River heading toward Bangor,	SPEED:	14 Knots

ROUTE: Boston - Bangor Line

PORTS: Boston, Rockland, Camden, Northport, Belfast, Searsport, Bucksport, Winterport, Hampden, Bangor.

COMPANY: Boston & Bangor Steamship Co.

LOCATION: On Penobscot River heading toward Bangor, from Hampden, Maine; Orrington Village in background.

OTHER NAME: *MOHAWK*

BUILT: 1882 - Smith & Townsend, East Boston, Massachusetts.

HISTORY: June 10, 1911, sold to McAllister Steamboat Co.
Renamed *MOHAWK*, March 22, 1912.
Manhattan Navigation Co., 1912 - 1915 (New York - Albany).

STATUS: 1917 converted to a schooner and sailed from New York, November, 1918. Was never heard from again.

BENEFACTOR

ROUTE:	Boston - Eastport - Way Ports.	NUMBER	2722
PORTS:	Boston, Eastport, Way Ports.	LENGTH:	173.0
COMPANY:	Clyde Steamship Co., of Maine.	BREADTH:	36.0
		DRAUGHT:	18.4
		GROSS TONNAGE:	843.55

BUILT: 1870 - Chester, Pennsylvania.

HISTORY: 1906-1907 Boston to Coast of Maine Canning Plants.
Later operated in freight service on Eastern's Bangor division with Captain A. E. Rawley in command.
He was later Flag Captain for Bangor Line, Eastern Steamship Co.

STATUS: Abandoned January 12, 1918, York Spit Light, Chesapeake Bay.

CAMDEN

ROUTE:	Boston - Bangor Line	NUMBER:	204087
PORTS:	Boston, Rockland, Camden, Belfast,	LENGTH:	320.5
	Bucksport, Winterport, Bangor	BREADTH:	40.0
COMPANY:	Eastern Steamship Lines, Inc.	DRAUGHT:	16.1
OTHER NAMES:	*COMET*, (Chinese) *WANSU*	GROSS TONNAGE:	2153.0
SISTER SHIP:	*BELFAST*	SPEED:	18 Knots
LOCATION:	Leaving Boston Harbor for Maine		
BUILT:	1907 - Bath Iron Works, Bath, Maine.		

HISTORY: Built for Bangor Line, used on International Line the first year in operation. During World War I, operated on the Boston - New York Line. Returned to Bangor Line. Unable to continue running to Maine after *MORRO CASTLE* loss, due to new navigation laws. Sold to Colonial Line April 8, 1936. Army Transport in Hawaiian Islands during World War II.

STATUS: April 30, 1948, sold to Asia Development Corp. of Shanghai.

James B. Vickery

BELFAST

ROUTE:	Boston - Bangor Line	NUMBER:	206266
PORTS:	Boston, Camden, Rockland, Belfast,	LENGTH:	320.6
	Bucksport, Winterport, Bangor.	BREADTH:	40.0
COMPANY:	Eastern Steamship Lines, Inc.	DRAUGHT:	16.1
OTHER NAME:	*ARROW*	GROSS TONNAGE:	2157.0
SISTER SHIP:	*CAMDEN*	SPEED:	18 Knots
LOCATION:	Proceeding up the Penobscot River.		
	View from Hampden shore.		
BUILT:	1909 - Bath Iron Works, Bath, Maine.		

HISTORY: Built for Bangor Line. Used on Boston - New York Line in World War I. Returned to Bangor Line until forced to cease operations due to strict navigation laws requiring double bottoms on all passenger ships. She and sister ship, *CAMDEN*, had single bottoms. Last sailing to Bangor, December, 1935. Sold to Colonial Line in 1936 for operation from Providence to New York. Used as United States Army Transport in Hawaiian Islands during World War II.

STATUS: While under tow from Puget Sound to Astoria in 1947, broke free, drifted on to beach at Astoria, Oregon. Total loss.

Chapter IF

Kennebec Line

Established in 1889 as the Kennebec Steamboat Company, the first ships used were the *SAGADAHOC* and the *KENNEBEC*. Later one was replaced by the propellor-driven *LINCOLN*, which did not meet the requirements of the service. The *RANSOM B. FULLER* was built for the service and used for a few years.

Eventually the line was served by the *CITY OF BANGOR* and the *CITY OF ROCKLAND*. They came to the Kennebec Line when the *CAMDEN* and the *BELFAST* were built.

Except for the *LINCOLN*, all Kennebec Line ships were paddel-wheel steamers.

The Kennebec Line became part of the Eastern Steamship Line in 1901.

SAGADAHOC

ROUTE:	Kennebec Line	NUMBER:	22151
PORTS:	Popham Beach, Bath, Richmond,	LENGTH:	244.2
	Dresden, Gardiner	BREADTH:	35.2
COMPANY:	Kennebec Steamboat Co.	DRAUGHT:	12.8
OTHER NAMES:	*STAR OF THE EAST, GREENPORT*	GROSS TONNAGE:	1413.0
LOCATION:	Boston Harbor, Massachusetts		
BUILT:	1866 - New York, New York.		

HISTORY: Rebuilt in 1889. Operated on Bangor Line and Kennebec Line until sold to run New York - Long Island Sound in 1903.
Finally New York to Troy, 1908 to 1913.

STATUS: Abandoned in New York Harbor (Harlem River), 1928.

R. B. Sanborn

KENNEBEC

ROUTE: Kennebec Line
PORTS: Popham Beach, Bath, Richmond,
Dresden, Gardiner
COMPANY: Kennebec Steamship Co.
OTHER NAME: *IROQUOIS*
LOCATION: Entering Gardiner on the Kennebec River.
BUILT: 1889 - New England Shipbuilding Co., Bath, Maine.
HISTORY: Used on the New York - Fall River Run of Enterprise Line in 1905. Acquired by McAllister Brothers in 1910.
Chartered to the Manhattan Line 1910-1915 (Hudson River Night Line).
STATUS: Burned at Elizabeth River after World War I.

NUMBER: 14484
LENGTH: 256.0
BREADTH: 37.6
DRAUGHT: 13.1
GROSS TONNAGE: 1652.0

LINCOLN

ROUTE:	Kennebec Line		NUMBER:	141499
PORTS:	Popham Beach, Bath, Richmond,		LENGTH:	203.4
	Dresden, Gardiner		BREADTH:	36.9
COMPANY:	Kennebec Steamboat Co.		DRAUGHT:	12.6
	Eastern Steamship Co.		GROSS TONNAGE:	997.0
OTHER NAMES:	*MARTINIQUE, KENTUCKY*			
LOCATION:	Turning in Kennebec River at Gardiner, Maine.			
BUILT:	1897 - New England Shipbuilding Co., Bath, Maine.			
HISTORY:	Sold to Peninsular & Occidental Co. Tampa - Havana Run.			
	Sold to Joy Line Providence - New York Run.			
	Sold to Pacific Coast owners, 1910.			
STATUS:	Foundered at sea on February 4, 1910, near Hatteras, South Carolina, while en route to West Coast.			

Mildred N. Thayer

CITY OF BANGOR (2)

ROUTE:	Kennebec Line	NUMBER:	127029
PORTS:	Popham Beach, Bath, Richmond,	LENGTH:	277.0
	Dresden, Gardiner	BREADTH:	38.0
COMPANY:	Eastern Steamship Lines, Inc.	DRAUGHT:	14.2
SISTER SHIP:	*CITY OF ROCKLAND*	GROSS TONNAGE:	1661.0
LOCATION:	Proceeding to dock in Bangor, Maine,	SPEED:	14 Knots
	on the Penobscot River.		

BUILT: 1894 - James McKie, Boston, Massachusetts.

HISTORY: Built for Bangor Line, used on Kennebec Line.
                 Later on Boston - Portland Line and last on Boston - Boothbay Line.

STATUS: Sank at Federal Wharf, East Boston, Massachusetts, December 27, 1933. Abandoned June 30,
                 1936.

CITY OF ROCKLAND

ROUTE:	Kennebec Line	NUMBER:	127545
PORTS:	Popham Beach, Bath, Richmond,	LENGTH:	277.0
	Dresden, Gardiner	BREADTH:	38.0
COMPANY:	Eastern Steamship Lines, Inc.	DRAUGHT:	14.2
SISTER SHIP:	*CITY OF BANGOR*	GROSS TONNAGE:	1696.0
LOCATION:	Sailing out of Boston Harbor,	SPEED:	14 Knots
	opposite the Merchants & Miners Piers.		
BUILT:	1901 - James McKie, Boston, Massachusetts,		
HISTORY:	Built for Bangor Line. Upon completion of *CAMDEN* and *BELFAST* operated on Kennebec Line.		
STATUS:	Wrecked September, 1923, at the mouth of the Kennebec River. Burned at Misery Island, Salem Harbor, October 27, 1924. Total loss.		

Chapter IG

Portland Line

This line began as the Portland Steam Packet Company in 1844 and joined the Eastern Steamship Company in 1901.

Most of the early vessels were paddle-wheel steamers including: *FOREST CITY, LEWISTON, TREMONT,* and *JOHN BROOKS*. These were later replaced by the *PORTLAND* and the *BAY STATE*.

After the loss of the *PORTLAND* in a bad storm, she was replaced by the new, steel, propellor-driven *GOVERNOR DINGLEY*.

Later the *RANSOM B. FULLER* was lengthened and the *BAY STATE* completely rebuilt. THese ships ran several years on the line.

The last few years of service was handled by the *CALVIN AUSTIN* and the *BRANDON*.

FOREST CITY

ROUTE:	Boston - Portland Line	NUMBER:	9513
PORTS:	Boston, Portland	LENGTH:	234.7
COMPANY:	Portland Steam Packet Co.	BREADTH:	33.0
SISTER SHIP:	*LEWISTON*	DRAUGHT:	9.8
		GROSS TONNAGE:	1134.33

BUILT: 1854 - John Englis & Son, Greenpoint, Long Island, New York.

HISTORY: Also on Portland, Rockland, Southwest Harbor, Jonesport Line.

STATUS: Dismantled at Nut Island, Quincy, Massachusetts, 1895.

LEWISTON

ROUTE:	Boston - Portland Line	NUMBER:	15084
PORTS:	Boston, Portland	LENGTH:	234.9
COMPANY:	Portland Steam Packet Co.	BREADTH:	33.1
SISTER SHIP:	*FOREST CITY*	DRAUGHT:	9.2
		GROSS TONNAGE:	1127.0

BUILT: 1856 - John Englis at New York.

HISTORY: Boston - Portland Line 1856-1867.
1867 sold to Portland, Mount Desert, and Machias Steamboat Co. 1884 sold to Maine Central Railroad with *CITY OF RICHMOND*.
1886 on Boston - Bangor Line, succeeding wrecked steamer, *CAMBRIDGE*.

STATUS: Broken up February, 1899.

TREMONT

ROUTE:	Boston - Portland Line	NUMBER:	145336
PORTS:	Boston, Portland	LENGTH:	260.0
COMPANY:	Portland Steam Packet Co.	BREADTH:	37.0
		DRAUGHT:	12.3
		GROSS TONNAGE:	1428.0

BUILT: 1883 - John Englis & Son, Greenpoint, New York,
HISTORY: Sold to Joy Line, March 20, 1901.
STATUS: Burned February 8, 1904, at Pier 35, East River, New York City. Scuttled to extinguish fire.

JOHN BROOKS

ROUTE:	Boston - Portland Line	NUMBER:	13452
PORTS:	Boston, Portland	LENGTH:	239.8
COMPANY:	Portland Steam Packet Co.	BREADTH:	31.4
		DRAUGHT:	10.8
		GROSS TONNAGE:	1011.0

BUILT: 1859 - New York

HISTORY: Ran on New York - Bridgeport Line.
            Purchased by Portland Steam Packet Co., 1865.
            Boston & Maine Steamship Co., Boston, Castine, Southwest Harbor, Bar Harbor, and Machiasport,
            1887.
            Ran on Boston - Bangor Line.
            1890-1894, Boston to Portsmouth, New Hampshire.

STATUS: Burned for old metal at Boston, Massachusetts, October, 1899.

PORTLAND

ROUTE:	Boston - Portland Line		NUMBER:	150488
PORTS:	Boston, Portland		LENGTH:	291.0
COMPANY:	Portland Steam Packet Co.		BREADTH:	42.1
SISTER SHIP:	*BAY STATE*		DRAUGHT:	15.5
			GROSS TONNAGE:	2283.0
			SPEED:	15 Knots

BUILT: 1890 - New England Shipbuilding Co., Bath, Maine.

HISTORY: Purser J. F. Hunt remained ashore in Boston on November 26, 1898, to attend the funeral of Captain Charles Deering. In paying respects to the deceased he avoided death himself. He served on the Boston - Portland Line until it was discontinued.

STATUS: Lost during hurricane November 26, 1898, off Cape Cod, Massachusetts.

BAY STATE

ROUTE:	Boston - Portland Line	NUMBER:	3645
PORTS:	Boston, Portland	LENGTH:	281.2
COMPANY:	Eastern Steamship Corp.	BREADTH:	42.1
SISTER SHIP:	*PORTLAND*	DRAUGHT:	15.5
LOCATION:	Sailing into Boston Harbor	GROSS TONNAGE:	2262.0

BUILT: 1896 - New England Shipbuilding Co., Bath, Maine.

HISTORY: Rebuilt 1910. Swept clean at main deck, everything above was new. Feathering paddle wheels installed, paddle shaft lowered, twenty-eight new state-rooms added.

STATUS: Lost near Portland Head, Cape Elizabeth, Maine, September 24, 1916.

RANSOM B. FULLER

ROUTE:	Boston - Portland	NUMBER:	111430
PORTS:	Boston, Portland	LENGTH:	317.5
COMPANY:	Eastern Steamship Lines, Inc.	BREADTH:	40.1
OTHER NAME:	*BROADWAY*	DRAUGHT:	14.0
LOCATION:	Sailing out of Boston Harbor, Massachusetts.	GROSS TONNAGE:	2329.0

BUILT: 1902 - New England Shipbuilding Co., Bath, Maine.

HISTORY: Built for Kennebec Line. In 1910 lengthened forty-five feet for Portland Line. Also ran a short time on Bangor Line and International Line.

STATUS: Wreckers started their work at Newburgh, New York, in 1935.

66

BRANDON

ROUTE:	Boston - Portland	NUMBER:	154469
PORTS:	Boston, Portland, Boothbay	LENGTH:	200.5
COMPANY:	Eastern Steamship Lines, Inc.	BREADTH:	37.0
OTHER NAMES:	*YONDAL, RIVIERE DE LOUP, SIMEON,*	DRAUGHT:	17.3
	MADELON II	GROSS TONNAGE:	1062.0
LOCATION:	Boothbay Harbor, Maine	SPEED:	12 Knots

BUILT: 1902 - Harlan & Hollingsworth Co., Wilmington, Delaware.

HISTORY: Built for Old Dominion Line, Norfolk - Richmond Run.
1925, Portland, Boothbay Harbor, Friendship, Rockland, Eastport, and Lubec. 1939, used in Quebec as *SIMEON*. 1951, registered under Honduran Flag.

STATUS: Sunk in Bickerdike Basin, Montreal, 8:30 a.m., November 22, 1968. Owned by Cie Navigation Voyageur Ltd.

Chapter IH

Small Eastern Vessels

Until the beginning of World War I the steamer *ST. ANDREWS* operated from Eastport and Lubec to St. Andrews and Calais.

The service from Rockland to Mount Desert Island and way stops was served by the *MOUNT DESERT* first, later the *J. T. MORSE*. The *CATHERINE, JULIETT,* and *BOOTHBAY* ran from Rockland to Blue Hill and way landings. These ships also ran in the fall and spring from Rockland to Mount Desert Island. Later the *SOUTHPORT* and *WESTPORT* ran from Rockland to Mount Desert Island and also from Rockland to Blue Hill.

During the summer the *MINEOLA* and *MONHEGAN* made a trip each way from Rockland to Portland, stopping at Tenants Harbor, Port Clyde, Friendship, Round Pond, New Harbor, Squirrel Island, Boothbay Harbor, and Southport and on to Portland.

The *DAMARIN, ISLAND BELLE, NAHANADA,* and *WIWURNA* ran from Bath to Boothbay and also on the Kennebec River.

The *BOOTHBAY*, originally built for this Line (but proved to be too large for the service), was followed by the *SOUTHPORT* and *WESTPORT,* which were also built for this line.

The *DELLA COLLINS*, a small stern paddle-wheel steamer operated from Bath to Richmond, Dresden, Gardiner, Hallowell, and Augusta. She ran on this route for a few years after being purchased. She was replaced by the new *CITY OF AUGUSTA*, also a stern paddle-wheel steamer.

Unlike the early steamship business on the West Coast, very few stern paddle-wheel steamers plied the New England waters.

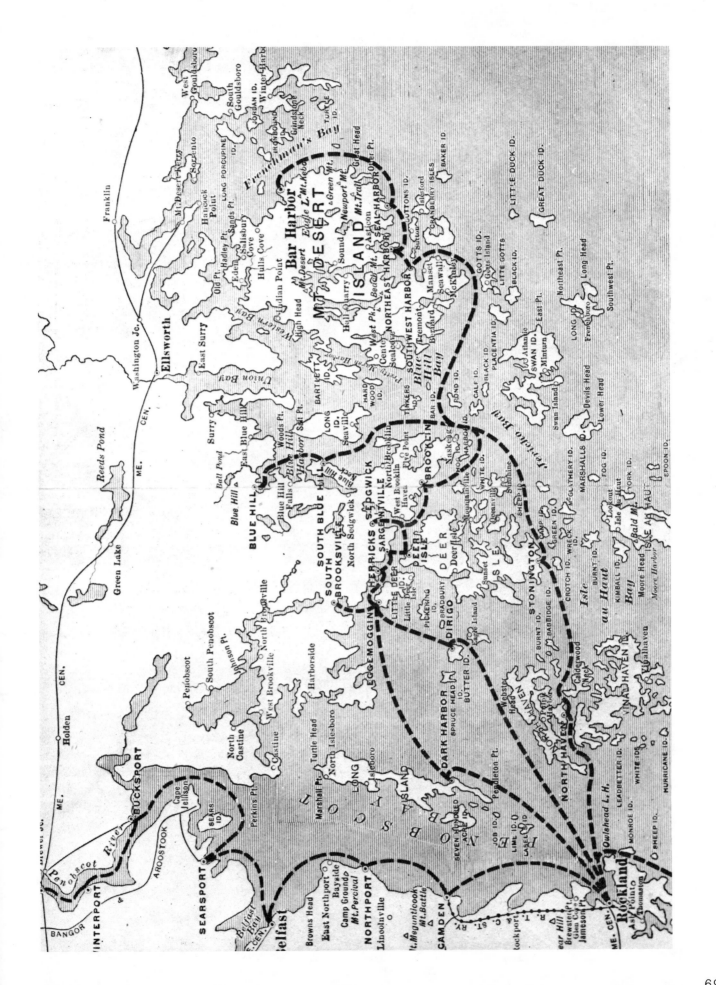

69

ST. ANDREWS

ROUTE:	St. Croix Line	NUMBER:	96564
PORTS:	Calais, St. Andrews, Eastport, Lubec	LENGTH:	113.6
COMPANY:	Eastern Steamship Co.	BREADTH:	27.2
OTHER NAMES:	*HENRY F. EATON, BRAS D'OR* (Canadian)	DRAUGHT:	8.9
LOCATION:	Calais Harbor, Maine	GROSS TONNAGE:	240.0
BUILT:	1901 - South Portland, Maine.		

HISTORY: Renamed *ST. ANDREWS* 1913; *BRAS D'OR* 1925.
Purchased by United States Government 1917. Sold to New York group for Hudson River service October 30, 1922. Sold to Sydney, Cape Breton, April 22, 1925. Owners Coastal Steamship Co., Ltd., Sydney, Nova Scotia, Canada.

MOUNT DESERT

ROUTE:	Rockland - Mount Desert Line	NUMBER:	91128
PORTS:	Rockland, North Haven, Stonington, Southwest	LENGTH:	162.0
	Harbor, Northeast Harbor, Seal Harbor, Bar Harbor	BREADTH:	27.0
COMPANY:	Boston & Bangor Steamship Co.	DRAUGHT:	9.6
OTHER NAME:	*ARION*	GROSS TONNAGE:	457.1
LOCATION:	En route from Bar Harbor, Maine,		
	to Seal Harbor, Maine.		
BUILT:	1879 - New England Shipbuilding Co., Bath, Maine.		
HISTORY:	Sold 1904 to run in Boston Harbor. Later in New York as part of Strain Fleet, running to Glen Island, New York.		
STATUS:	Condemned 1913, Edgewater, New Jersey.		

A. B. Sides

J. T. MORSE

ROUTE:	Rockland - Mount Desert Line	NUMBER:	200980
PORTS:	Rockland, North Haven, Stonington,	LENGTH:	214.0
	Southwest Harbor, Manset, Northeast Harbor,	BREADTH:	31.0
	Seal Harbor, Bar Harbor	DRAUGHT:	12.1
COMPANY:	Eastern Steamship Lines Inc.	GROSS TONNAGE:	780.0
OTHER NAME:	*YANKEE*	SPEED:	16.5 Knots
LOCATION:	Entering Bar Harbor, Maine		
BUILT:	1904 - William McKie, East Boston, Massachusetts.		
HISTORY:	Maine 1904-1931; New York Harbor 1933-1939.		
STATUS:	Condemned 1941 at Athens, New York. Broken up at Rossville, Staten Island, New York, 1942.		

CATHERINE

ROUTE: Rockland - Blue Hill Line

PORTS: Rockland, Dark Harbor, Eggemoggin,
                Sargentville, Deer Isle, Sedgewick,
                Brooklyn, South Brooksville, West Tremont
                South Blue Hill, and Blue Hill

COMPANY: Eastern Steamship Corp.

OTHER NAMES: *NAHANT* (2), *ONEIDA, OAKLAND BEACH*

LOCATION: Penobscot River Area.

BUILT: 1893 - C. B. Harrington, Bath, Maine.

HISTORY: 1924, purchased by Dickson Steamship Co. for Boston - Nahant Run. Sold to Oakland Beach Ferry
                Service of New York, 1928.

STATUS: Broken up 1930.

NUMBER: 126971
LENGTH: 100.4
BREADTH: 18.1
DRAUGHT: 8.1
GROSS TONNAGE: 161.0

JULIETTE

ROUTE:	Rockland - Blue Hill Line	NUMBER:	77035
PORTS:	Rockland, Dark Harbor, Eggemoggin,	LENGTH:	95.6
	Sargentville, Deer Isle, Sedgewick,	BREADTH:	23.1
	Brooklin, South Brooksville, West Tremont,	DRAUGHT:	7.5
	South Blue Hill, and Blue Hill.	GROSS TONNAGE:	132.0
COMPANY:	Eastern Steamship Corp.		
OTHER NAME:	*ISLAND BELLE*		
LOCATION:	Penobscot River Area.		
BUILT:	1892 - Bath, Maine.		
HISTORY:	1920-21 ran from Providence, Rhode Island, to Newport, Rhode Island, as *ISLAND BELLE*.		
STATUS:	Broke up and sank off Florida Keys, 1925.		

BOOTHBAY

ROUTE:	Rockland - Blue Hill Line	NUMBER:	204233
PORTS:	Rockland, Dark Harbor, Eggemoggin,	LENGTH:	126.6
	South Brooksville, Sargentville, Deer Isle,	BREADTH:	33.0
	Brooklin, South Blue Hill, Blue Hill.	DRAUGHT:	10.0
COMPANY:	Eastern Steamship Lines, Inc.	GROSS TONNAGE:	343.0

OTHER NAMES: *GRAMPUS, DEEP WATER, LIBERTY*
LOCATION: Stonington Harbor, Maine
BUILT: 1907 - Neafie & Levy Ship and Engine Co., Philadelphia, Pennsylvania.
HISTORY: Built for Bath - Boothbay Line but was unable to successfully dock at small landings.
1962, used on Statue of Liberty Run.
1966, Boston - Provincetown Run.

SOUTHPORT

ROUTE:	Bath - Boothbay Service	NUMBER:	208730
PORTS:	Bath, Westport, Robinhood, MacMahan	LENGTH:	125.6
	Island, Five Islands, Sawyer's Island,	BREADTH:	21.2
	Isle of Springs, Southport, Capital Island,	DRAUGHT:	8.8
	Squirrel Island, Boothbay Harbor, Christmas Cove.	GROSS TONNAGE:	245.0
COMPANY:	Eastern Steamship Co.	SPEED:	12 Knots
OTHER NAME:	*COLONEL FRANK H. ADAMS*		
SISTER SHIP:	*WESTPORT*		
BUILT:	1911 - Wm. McKie, Boston, Massachusetts.		
HISTORY:	Built for Bath - Boothbay Run. Used Summers on Rockland - Blue Hill Line. 1950, used for excursions around Manhattan Island. Used by United States Army in World Wars I and II.		

WESTPORT

ROUTE:	Rockland - Blue Hill	NUMBER:	208731
PORTS:	Rockland, Dark Harbor, Eggemoggin,	LENGTH:	125.6
	South Brooksville, Sargentville, Deer Isle,	BREADTH:	21.2
	Brooklin, South Blue Hill, Blue Hill.	DRAUGHT:	8.8
COMPANY:	Eastern Steamship Lines, Inc.	GROSS TONNAGE:	246.0

OTHER NAMES: *COLONEL LOUIS F. GARRARD,*
U.S.S. ADAMS

SISTER SHIP: *SOUTHPORT*

BUILT: 1911 - Wm. McKie, Boston, Massachusetts.

HISTORY: Built for Bath - Boothbay Line. Ran most of her life in Maine on Rockland - Blue Hill Line and Rockland - Mount Desert Line. Used in World Wars I and II by the United States Army. 1950, used for excursions out of Boston Harbor. 1956, used for excursions out of Newark, New Jersey.

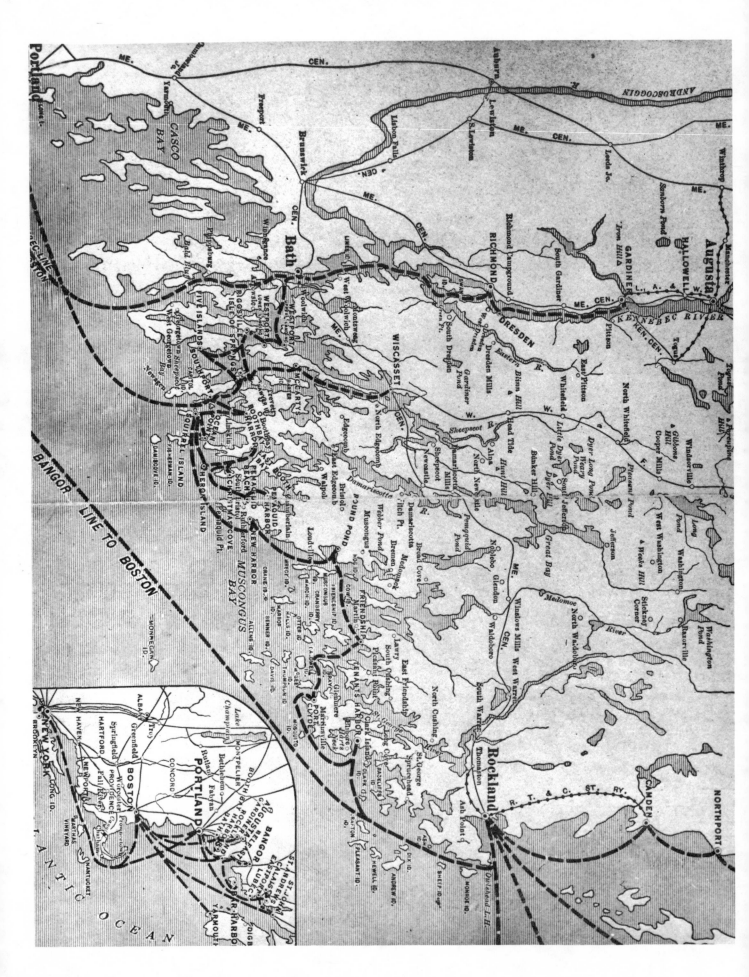

MINEOLA

ROUTE:	Portland - Rockland Line	NUMBER:	93131
PORTS:	Rockland, Tenants Harbor, Port Clyde,	LENGTH:	121.0
	Friendship, Round Pond, New Harbor, Squirrel	BREADTH:	26.0
	Island, Boothbay Harbor, Southport, Portland.	DRAUGHT:	9.6
COMPANY:	Eastern Steamship Co.	GROSS TONNAGE:	367.0
LOCATION:	Off Tenants Harbor, Maine		
BUILT:	1901 - Port Clyde, Maine.		

HISTORY: Eastern Steamship Co. took over *MINEOLA* and *MONHEGAN* in order to furnish service each way every day starting in 1906.

STATUS: During a gale drifted on a ledge and sank at Pawtucket, Rhode Island, 1929.

MONHEGAN

ROUTE:	Portland - Rockland Line	NUMBER:	93395
PORTS:	Portland, Southport, Boothbay Harbor,	LENGTH:	128.0
	Squirrel Island, New Harbor, Round Pond,	BREADTH:	26.7
	Friendship, Port Clyde, Tenants Harbor,	DRAUGHT:	11.2
	Rockland.	GROSS TONNAGE:	387.0
COMPANY:	Eastern Steamship Co.		
BUILT:	1903 - Cobb-Butler Yard, Rockland, Maine.		
HISTORY:	Sold by Eastern Steamship Lines, Inc., to Blackstone Valley Transportation Co. in Rhode Island, August 6, 1919.		
STATUS:	Wrecked during 1938 hurricane in Providence, Rhode Island.		

DAMARIN

ROUTE:	Bath - Boothbay Line	NUMBER:	115163
PORTS:	Kennebec River and Boothbay Harbor	LENGTH:	67.6
	Region Stops	BREADTH:	13.7
COMPANY:	Eastern Steamboat Co.	DRAUGHT:	7.2
OTHER NAME:	*SAMOSET*	GROSS TONNAGE:	55.0
BUILT:	1873 - Bath, Maine.		
HISTORY:	Popham Beach - Bath Run, 1899-1903.		
STATUS:	Abandoned June 30, 1921.		

F. E. Claes

ISLAND BELLE

ROUTE:	Kennebec River - Boothbay Harbor		NUMBER:	100490
PORTS:	Kennebec River, Boothbay Region Stops		LENGTH:	93.0
COMPANY:	Eastern Steamboat Co.		BREADTH:	18.4
			DRAUGHT:	7.5
			GROSS TONNAGE:	153.0

BUILT: 1891 - Buffalo, New York.

HISTORY: Sold to Portland parties in 1911. Used in Casco Bay Service. Sold to Boston owners, 1917.

STATUS: Abandoned 1927, Boston, Massachusetts.

NAHANADA

ROUTE: Bath - Boothbay Line
PORTS: Bath, Boothbay Region
COMPANY: Eastern Steamship Co.

NUMBER:	130416
LENGTH:	89.0
BREADTH:	20.6
DRAUGHT:	7.5
GROSS TONNAGE:	91.0
SPEED:	14 Knots

BUILT: 1888 - New England Shipbuilding Co., Bath, Maine.
HISTORY: First triple expansion engine in the United States.
STATUS: Abandoned June 30, 1931.

WIWURNA

ROUTE:	Bath - Boothbay Line	NUMBER:	81043
PORTS:	Bath, Boothbay Region	LENGTH:	101.5
COMPANY:	Eastern Steamship Co.	BREADTH:	19.2
LOCATION:	Boothbay Harbor, Maine	DRAUGHT:	7.5
		GROSS TONNAGE:	98.0

BUILT: 1884 - Wm. Rogers Yard, Bath, Maine.

HISTORY: August 22, 1889, President Benjamin Harrison was a passenger. September 18, 1925, last trip from Bath to Boothbay piloted by the famous Captain Ross Dickson.

STATUS: Abandoned 1933, Portland, Maine.

CITY OF AUGUSTA

ROUTE: Kennebec River
PORTS: Bath, Augusta on Kennebec River
COMPANY: Eastern Steamship Co.
OTHER NAME: *ST. JOHNS*

NUMBER: 202891
LENGTH: 150.0
BREADTH: 31.3
DRAUGHT: 6.5
GROSS TONNAGE: 330.0

BUILT: 1906 - Boston, Massachusetts.
HISTORY: Built to replace *DELLA COLLINS*. Ran on Kennebec River until 1915. Tied up at Southport for several years. Sold November, 1917, to Jacksonville, Florida, interests. Ran on St. Johns River, Florida, between Jacksonville and Palatka. Only stern wheel ship built by the Eastern Steamship Co.
STATUS: Destroyed by fire in Savannah, Georgia.

Chapter 2

Maine Central Railroad Fleet

Some of the best steamers of any of the railroad fleets on the Atlantic coast were in this fleet. This was especially true of the *MOOSEHEAD* and the *RANGELEY*. When originated several ships ran on the coast as extensions of railroad Lines. The influence of the Eastern Railroad, running from Boston to Portland, with a controlling interest in the Maine Central Railroad, resulted in the establishment of the service handled by the *CITY OF RICHMOND* from 1867 to 1893, followed by the *FRANK JONES* from 1892 to 1905.

This service, at first, ran from Portland to Rockland, on to Mount Desert Island, ending at Machiasport after making several stops. When the Maine Central Railroad completed its line from Brunswick to Rockland, this service terminated at Rockland. When the Washington County Railroad line was built from Ellsworth to Downeast, serving Machias, the railroad steamship service was discontinued.

Other services of the Maine Central Railroad were extensions from Rockland to stops on islands where railroad lines were an impossibility. One of the important summer lines was from Rockland to Dark Harbor and Castine. Also, the service from Mount Desert Ferry in Hancock to Bar Harbor, Seal Harbor, Northeast Harbor, Southwest Harbor, and Manset was helpful in maintaining the most important summer colonies in the State of Maine. At one time it was acknowledged, that passengers served by the two lines during July and August, had more wealth than any concentration of summer people at other resorts in the United States.

Although the ships remained in service long after automobiles became a way of life, they operated only until 1931.

Steamers shown in this group are: *CITY OF RICHMOND, FRANK JONES, SEBENOA, SAPPHO, SAMOSET, NORUMBEGA, SIEUR DE MONTS, PEMAQUID,* and *RANGELEY.*

CITY OF RICHMOND

			NUMBER:	5020
ROUTE:	Portland - Rockland - Machias Line		LENGTH:	227.5
PORTS:	Portland, Machiasport, Way Stops		BREADTH:	30.6
COMPANY:	Maine Central Railroad Co.		DRAUGHT:	10.0
OTHER NAME:	*CITY OF KEY WEST*		GROSS TONNAGE:	875.0

BUILT: 1865 - Norton & Edmunds, Athens, New York.

HISTORY: Bought by Maine Central Railroad Co., September 25, 1884. Renamed *CITY OF KEY WEST* 1896.
Home ports:
Hudson, New York - 1865-1866.
Portland, Maine - April 24, 1866-June, 1893.
New London, Connecticut - 1893-1896.
St. Augustine, Florida - 1896-1901.
New Haven, Connecticut - 1901-1903.
New York City - 1903-1908.

STATUS: Broken up 1908.

Amos W. Kimball

FRANK JONES

ROUTE:	Portland - Rockland - Machias Line	NUMBER:	120903
PORTS:	Way Ports, Portland, Machias, via	LENGTH:	263.2
	Eggemoggin Reach	BREADTH:	36.3
COMPANY:	Maine Central Railroad Co.	DRAUGHT:	13.8
OTHER NAME:	*FENIMORE*	GROSS TONNAGE:	1634.0

BUILT: 1892 - New England Shipbuilding Co., Bath, Maine. Engine by Bath Iron Works.

HISTORY: One of the earliest ships to be electrically equipped.
Sold for New York - Fall River Line Run, May 25, 1905.
New Hudson River Line, 1908-1918.
Chartered by United States Navy, April, 1918.

STATUS: Completely destroyed by ammunition explosion, June 22, 1918, Norfolk, Virginia.

SEBENOA

ROUTE:	Bar Harbor Ferry	NUMBER:	115704
PORTS:	Mount Desert Ferry to Bar Harbor	LENGTH:	91.0
COMPANY:	Maine Central Railroad Co.	BREADTH:	18.6
LOCATION:	Off Bar Harbor, Maine	DRAUGHT:	7.2
		GROSS TONNAGE:	89.0

BUILT: 1880 - Bath, Maine.

HISTORY: Sold by Eastern Steamboat Co., Bath, Maine, March 27, 1884, to Maine Central Railroad Co. First steamer of Mount Desert Ferry Service.
Sold by Maine Central Railroad Co., 1911, to Vinalhaven & Rockland Steamboat Co.
Made into Towboat at Bridgeport, Connecticut, 1920.

STATUS: Abandoned, 1928.

W. H. Ballard

SAPPHO

ROUTE: Bar Harbor Ferry
PORTS: Mount Desert Ferry, Hancock Point, Bar Harbor, Seal Harbor, Northeast Harbor, Manset, Southwest Harbor
COMPANY: Maine Central Railroad Co.
OTHER NAME: *PAWTUCKET*
LOCATION: Entering Bar Harbor, Maine
BUILT: 1886 - Bath, Maine.
HISTORY: Left Maine Central Railroad Co. in 1916.
STATUS: Stripped during World War II due to age. Abandoned, 1948.

NUMBER: 116098
LENGTH: 149.18
BREADTH: 28.8
DRAUGHT: 9.5
GROSS TONNAGE: 275.0

SAMOSET

ROUTE:	Winter, Rockland - Castine	NUMBER:	107304
PORTS:	Rockland, Castine	LENGTH:	103.3
COMPANY:	Maine Central Railroad Co.	BREADTH:	23.0
OTHER NAMES:	*ANNIE L. VANSEIVER, EVERGLADES,*	DRAUGHT:	7.6
	CITY OF PUNTA GORDA, SEMINOLE	GROSS TONNAGE:	294.0

BUILT:　　　　1897 - Philadelphia, Pennsylvania.

HISTORY:　　　Started Maine Central Railroad Co., 1905. Sold to United States Navy, 1918. New York area, 1922-1923, as *EVERGLADES*. Florida as *CITY OF PUNTA GORDA*, 1927. New York area, 1930-1932 as *SEMINOLE*.

STATUS:　　　Sunk off Cape Charles, Virginia, by steamer, *ELISHA LEE*.

NORUMBEGA

ROUTE:	Bar Harbor Ferry	NUMBER:	130979
PORTS:	Mount Desert Ferry, Hancock Point,	LENGTH:	146.0
	Sorrento, Bar Harbor, Seal Harbor,	BREADTH:	28.6
	Northeast Harbor, Manset, Southwest Harbor	DRAUGHT:	10.1
COMPANY:	Maine Central Railroad Co.	GROSS TONNAGE:	304.0
OTHER NAME:	*ROMANCE*		
BUILT:	1902 - Bath, Maine.		
HISTORY:	Left Maine Central Railroad Co. in 1928. Sailed excursion routes out of Boston until destroyed by fire.		
STATUS:	Burned at Quincy, Massachusetts, May 20, 1934, Maine steamer *MAY ARCHER* burned also.		

SIEUR DE MONTS

ROUTE:	Rockland - Castine	NUMBER:	20633
PORTS:	Rockland, Dark Harbor, Castine	LENGTH:	155.5
COMPANY:	Maine Central Railroad Co.	BREADTH:	32.0
OTHER NAMES:	*QUAKER CITY, GENERAL L'ENFANT,*	DRAUGHT:	7.4
	GENERAL MATHEWS	GROSS TONNAGE:	469.0

BUILT: 1901 - Neafie & Levy, Philadelphia, Pennsylvania.

HISTORY: Sold to Maine Central Railroad Co., October 8, 1905.
                 Sold by Maine Central Railroad Co., September 12, 1917.
                 Renamed *GENERAL L'ENFANT*. Renamed *GENERAL MATHEWS*, 1923.

STATUS: Burned at Norfolk, Virginia, March 22, 1930. Later converted to oil barge.

PEMAQUID

ROUTE:	Rockland - Castine		NUMBER:	141270
PORTS:	1909 - Rockland, North Haven, Stonington,		LENGTH:	132.5
	Brooklin, Sedgewick, Deer Isle, Sargentville.		BREADTH:	28.0
	1918 - Rockland, Dark Harbor, Castine.		DRAUGHT:	9.8
COMPANY:	Maine Central Railroad Co.		GROSS TONNAGE:	420.0
OTHER NAMES:	*LONG ISLAND, U.S.S. MAJOR JACOB,*			
	ALONZO HOWE			
LOCATION:	Turning in Stonington Harbor, Maine.			
BUILT:	1893 - Neafie & Levy, Philadelphia, Pennsylvania.			
HISTORY:	Long Island Railroad, 1893-1901.			
	Maine Central Railroad, 1901-1931.			
STATUS:	Operating at Long Island, 1956.			

The Peabody Museum of Salem

MOOSEHEAD

ROUTE: Bar Harbor Ferry - Mount Desert Island
PORTS: Mount Desert Ferry, Hancock Point,
Bar Harbor, Seal Harbor, Northeast Harbor,
Manset, Southwest Harbor.
COMPANY: Maine Central Railroad Co.
OTHER NAMES: *PORPOISE, MAYFLOWER,*
COLONEL WILLIAM B. CORWIN
SISTER SHIP: *RANGELEY*
LOCATION: At Bar Harbor, Maine.
BUILT: 1911 - Bath Iron Works, Bath, Maine.
HISTORY: Left Maine Central Railroad 1919. **Note:** This steamer was probably the finest railroad passenger
steamer on the Atlantic Coast.
STATUS: Stranded December 17, 1941, off Boston, Massachusetts. Total loss.

NUMBER: 208616
LENGTH: 185.3
BREADTH: 35.8
DRAUGHT: 13.9
GROSS TONNAGE: 677.0
SPEED: 20 Knots

RANGELEY

ROUTE: Bar Harbor Ferry - Mount Desert Island
PORTS: Mount Desert Ferry, Hancock Point,
                Bar Harbor, Seal Harbor, Northeast
                Harbor, Manset, Southwest Harbor.
COMPANY: Maine Central Railroad Co.
OTHER NAMES: *CHAUNCEY M. DEPEW, SOMERS ISLE* (British)
SISTER SHIP: *MOOSEHEAD*
BUILT: 1913 - Bath Iron Works, Bath, Maine.
HISTORY: Left Maine Central Railroad Co., May 5, 1925. Sold to Hudson River Day Line, ran 1925-1940.
HISTORY: Chartered to United States Government, 1940. 1942, requisitioned by War Shipping Administration. Ran as excursion ship after World War II from Boston to Provincetown, Providence to Block Island, New York City to Atlantic Highlands. 1950, owned by Government of Bermuda. Crew Ship Tender in Hamilton, Bermuda, 1964.
STATUS: Purchased to be used as restaurant in New Jersey.

NUMBER: 211290
LENGTH: 185.1
BREADTH: 35.6
DRAUGHT: 13.5
GROSS TONNAGE: 652.0
SPEED: 18 Knots

Chapter 3

Swans Island and Vinalhaven Fleet

The Rockland & Vinalhaven Steamboat Company's fleet serviced two routes: Vinalhaven to Rockland, making two round trips a day in the summer, and one in the winter; Swans Island service, leaving Swans Island and stopping at Stonington, North Haven, and Rockland, returning in the afternoon to Swans Island with way stops. As a special accommodation to residents of Isle au Haut, the Swans Island steamer would make an afternoon call several times during the summer. The Swans Island steamer serviced Vinalhaven and North Haven during the severe winters.

The following ships were used: *CLARA CLARITA, MAY FIELD, EMMELINE, FOREST QUEEN*, SEBENOA*, VINALHAVEN, GOVERNOR BODWELL, NORTH HAVEN, W. S. WHITE, VINALHAVEN II,* and *NORTH HAVEN II.*

The first service from Rockland to Vinalhaven had a very exciting history. Several steamship companies were formed, competing with each other. Out of this emerged the final company. In recent years the *VINALHAVEN* ran from Vinalhaven to Rockland, and the *GOVERNOR BODWELL* ran from Swans Island to Rockland. After the loss of the *GOVERNOR BODWELL*, the service was handled by the *NORTH HAVEN*. The *W. S. WHITE* replaced the *VINALHAVEN* when advanced age forced her retirement. The *VINALHAVEN II* and the *NORTH HAVEN II* provided service to the area for a few years during World War II. The service today is provided by State of Maine owned automobile ferries.

* Pictures of the *SEBENOA* and the *FOREST QUEEN* are shown in Chapters 2 and 7.

CLARA CLARITA

ROUTE:	Rockland - Vinalhaven	NUMBER:	4873
PORTS:	Rockland, Vinalhaven	LENGTH:	115.0
COMPANY:	Rockland & Vinalhaven Steamboat Co.	BREADTH:	22.8
		DRAUGHT:	19.0
		GROSS TONNAGE:	125.15

BUILT: 1864 - Brooklyn, New York.
HISTORY: 1879-1881 at Rockland, Maine. Rebuilt for tug use at Portland, Maine, 1881.
STATUS: Abandoned 1908.

Deer Isle - Stonington Historical Society

MAY FIELD

ROUTE: Rockland - Vinalhaven Line
PORTS: Rockland, Vinalhaven
COMPANY: Bangor & Bar Harbor Steamboat Co.
LOCATION: Rockland Harbor, Maine

NUMBER: 90753
LENGTH: 73.5
BREADTH: 13.2
DRAUGHT: 4.0
GROSS TONNAGE: 48.62

BUILT: 1875 - Barbour Brothers, Brewer, Maine.
HISTORY: Ran out of Rockland all her life.
STATUS: Owned by Bodwell Granite Co. Total wreck about 1893 on Maine Coast.

Deer Isle - Stonington Historical Society

EMMELINE

ROUTE: Rockland - Vinalhaven Line
PORTS: Rockland, Vinalhaven
COMPANY: Rockland & Vinalhaven Steamboat Co.

BUILT: 1890 - Ashtabula, Ohio.
HISTORY: Rockland, 1891-1893.
STATUS: Abandoned June 30, 1932.

NUMBER: 136133
LENGTH: 116.91
BREADTH: 22.9
DRAUGHT: 6.9
GROSS TONNAGE: 116.91

VINALHAVEN

ROUTE:	Rockland - Vinalhaven Line	NUMBER:	161690
PORTS:	Rockland, Vinalhaven, North Haven,	LENGTH:	115.4
	Stonington, Swans Island	BREADTH:	16.0
COMPANY:	Vinalhaven & Rockland Steamboat Co.	DRAUGHT:	7.3
LOCATION:	Tied up at Tillson's Wharf,	GROSS TONNAGE:	186.0
	Rockland Harbor, Maine		
BUILT:	1892 - Searsport, Maine, July 2.		

HISTORY: Ran entire life from Rockland to Vinalhaven or on Rockland - Swans Island Line. A large naval vessel, on the trial course off Rockland before World War II, nearly swamped the ship. Waves put the fire out in the boilers.

STATUS: Sold, stripped of equipment and abandoned August, 1938, Rockland, Maine.

GOVERNOR BODWELL

ROUTE:	Swans Island Line	NUMBER:	86215
PORTS:	Rockland, North Haven, Stonington,	LENGTH:	103.0
	Isle au Haut, Swans Island	BREADTH:	24.0
COMPANY:	Vinalhaven - Rockland Steamboat Co.	DRAUGHT:	8.2
LOCATION:	Backing away from a dock at	GROSS TONNAGE:	170.0
	Rockland, Maine		
BUILT:	1892 - Rockland, Maine.		
HISTORY:	Ran entire life either from Rockland to Swans Island or Rockland to Vinalhaven.		
STATUS:	Burned at a Swans Island wharf March 23, 1931.		

NORTH HAVEN

ROUTE:	Swans Island Line		NUMBER:	230975
PORTS:	Rockland, North Haven, Stonington,		LENGTH:	108.0
	Swans Island		BREADTH:	23.5
COMPANY:	Vinalhaven & Rockland Steamboat Co.		DRAUGHT:	9.6
OTHER NAMES:	*ELECTRONIC, MANHATTAN*		GROSS TONNAGE:	210.0
LOCATION:	Sailing from Rockland, Maine		SPEED:	12 Knots
BUILT:	1913 - South Portland, Maine.			

HISTORY: Used at Sydney, Cape Breton, Nova Scotia, prior to services in Maine. Purchased 1931 to replace burned *GOVERNOR BODWELL*. Used in World War II by United States Navy to transport sailors from warships in Casco Bay to dock in Portland. Sold July 30, 1946, to J. Driscoll of New York. Sold to Circle Line, New York, October, 1956.

STATUS: Laid up 1961.

R. Loren Graham

W. S. WHITE

ROUTE: Vinalhaven Line
PORTS: Rockland, Vinalhaven
COMPANY: Vinalhaven & Rockland Steamboat Co.
OTHER NAMES: *GOSNOLD, MIRAMAR, CARIBBEAN*
LOCATION: In Rockland Harbor, Maine

NUMBER: 203183
LENGTH: 103.0
BREADTH: 24.3
DRAUGHT: 9.4
GROSS TONNAGE: 221.0
SPEED: 13 Knots

BUILT: 1906 - Palmer Steamboat Co., Noank, Connecticut.
HISTORY: Cuttyhunk Line 1906-1917. United States Army 1917-1921. New York area 1921-1934. Vinalhaven Line 1934-1942.
STATUS: In Port of Spain, Trinidad, after 1944.

W. H. Ballard

VINALHAVEN II

ROUTE: Vinalhaven Line
PORTS: Rockland, Vinalhaven
COMPANY: Vinalhaven Port District, Inc.

BUILT: 1943 - Southwest Harbor, Maine
HISTORY: Sold to Boston purchaser, May 2, 1959.
STATUS: Running in Boston 1980.

NUMBER: 243818
LENGTH: 60.3
BREADTH: 18.3
DRAUGHT: 7.3
GROSS TONNAGE: 57.0

NORTH HAVEN II

ROUTE:	Rockland - North Haven	NUMBER:	249656
PORTS:	Rockland, North Haven	LENGTH:	58.1
COMPANY:	Town of North Haven, Maine	BREADTH:	17.1
OTHER NAME:	*T-12* (USA)	DRAUGHT:	18.4
LOCATION:	Dock at North Haven, Maine	GROSS TONNAGE:	47.0
BUILT:	1942 - Stonington, Maine.		
HISTORY:	1946-1960 Rockland - North Haven, Maine.		

Chapter 4

Passamaquoddy Vessels

FLUSHING and *AURORA (GRAND MANAN)* were operated by the Grand Manan Steamboat Company between Grand Manan, Eastport, Lubec, St. Andrews, and Saint John. They were followed by *GRAND MANAN II*, owned by the Eastern Coastal Steamship Company. The Frontier Steamboat Company operated between Calais, St. Andrews, Eastport, and Lubec using the steamers *CHARLES HOUGHTON, JEANETTE*, and *ROSE STANDISH*.

Other ships running the same route during this time were *VIKING* and *CURLEW*.

From 1901 to 1917 the Eaton family operated the *HENRY F. EATON*. This ship later became the Eastern Steamship Company's *ST. ANDREWS*.

The Passamaquoddy Ferry and Navigation Company operated between Eastport and Lubec, making several stops at Campobello Island. The steamers *LUBEC* and *EASTPORT* were used.

FLUSHING (Canadian)

ROUTE:	New Brunswick, Maine, Grand Manan Island	NUMBER:	120526
PORTS:	Saint John, St. Stephen, St. Andrews,	LENGTH:	112.0
	Eastport, Campobello, Welch Pool,	BREADTH:	24.0
	Grand Manan Island	DRAUGHT:	8.2
COMPANY:	Grand Manan Steamboat Co., Ltd.	GROSS TONNAGE:	217.0
BUILT:	1882 - Athens, New York.		

HISTORY: First regular ferry to Grand Manan Island. Purchased 1884. Rebuilt in 1908, Saint John, New Brunswick. Formerly ran from Flushing, Long Island, to New York City.

STATUS: Sold to be converted to tugboat.

AURORA (Canadian)

ROUTE:	New Brunswick, Maine, Grand Manan Island	NUMBER:	107036
PORTS:	Saint John, St. Stephen, St. Andrews,	LENGTH:	114.8
	Eastport, Campobello, Welch Pool,	BREADTH:	26.6
	Grand Manan Island.	DRAUGHT:	10.9
COMPANY:	Grand Manan Steamboat Co., Ltd.	GROSS TONNAGE:	297.0
OTHER NAME:	*GRAND MANAN*		
BUILT:	1893 - Brooklyn, New York		
HISTORY:	In service 1900-1930. Rebuilt and renamed *GRAND MANAN*, 1911.		

GRAND MANAN II (Canadian)

ROUTE:	New Brunswick, Grand Manan Island, New Brunswick	NUMBER:	156702
		LENGTH:	144.3
PORTS:	Saint John, St. Andrews, Wilson's Beach, Grand Manan Island	BREADTH:	32.1
		DRAUGHT:	12.5
COMPANY:	Eastern Canada Coastal Steamship Co.	GROSS TONNAGE:	841.0
BUILT:	Saint John Shipbuilding & Drydock Co., Ltd., Saint John, New Brunswick.		
HISTORY:	Began service February, 1930. Nicknamed *IRON DUKE*. Sold during World War II to Canadian Government.		

CHARLES HOUGHTON

ROUTE: Eastport - Calais
PORTS: Eastport, Calais, Way Ports
COMPANY: Frontier Steamboat Co.
LOCATION: Calais Harbor, Maine

NUMBER: 4253
LENGTH: 133.0
BREADTH: 32.4
DRAUGHT: 9.0
GROSS TONNAGE: 282.0

BUILT: 1863 - McKay & Aldus, Boston, Massachusetts.
HISTORY: Boston - Gloucester Run after end of Civil War.
STATUS: Burned, December 30, 1891, at a wharf in Calais, Maine.

111

ROSE STANDISH

ROUTE:	Eastport, Maine - St. Andrews, New Brunswick - Calais, Maine		NUMBER:	21130
			LENGTH:	151.1
PORTS:	Eastport, Calais, Way Ports		BREADTH:	27.4
COMPANY:	Frontier Steamboat Co., Calais, Maine		DRAUGHT:	8.1
LOCATION:	Calais Harbor, Maine		GROSS TONNAGE:	393.0
BUILT:	1863 - Lawrence & Saukes, Brooklyn, New York.			
HISTORY:	1863-1887 for Boston & Hingham Steamboat Co. 1887 sold to Frontier Steamboat Co. During Civil War, chartered by United States Government. Used to exchange prisoners.			
STATUS:	Totally destroyed by fire April 20, 1900, at a wharf in Calais, Maine.			

Cecil J. Miller

VIKING

ROUTE: Eastport - Calais
PORTS: Eastport, Calais, Way Ports

NUMBER: 161645
LENGTH: 75.3
BREADTH: 15.2
DRAUGHT: 6.4
GROSS TONNAGE: 120.24

BUILT: 1891 - Ashtabula, Ohio.
HISTORY: Belfast to Castine, 1892-1896.
Campobello, Canada, area, 1896-1909.
STATUS: Abandoned at Deer Isle, Maine, 1909.

Cecil J. Miller

CURLEW

ROUTE: Calais - Eastport Line
PORTS: Calais, Eastport, Way Ports

BUILT: 1895 - Milbridge, Maine.

NUMBER: 127080
LENGTH: 59.4
BREADTH: 14.6
DRAUGHT: 6.0
GROSS TONNAGE: 29.0

JEANETTE

ROUTE:	Eastport - Calais	NUMBER:	77090
PORTS:	Eastport, Calais, Way Ports	LENGTH:	80.5
COMPANY:	Frontier Steamboat Co.	BREADTH:	19.6
OTHER NAMES:	*MORRIS BLOCK, KINGSTON*	DRAUGHT:	5.4
		GROSS TONNAGE:	73.64

BUILT:	1893 - Norwalk, Florida.
HISTORY:	1893 - Jacksonville, Florida.
	1894 - Boston, Massachusetts.
	1896-1903 - Calais, Maine.
	1904 - Salem, Massachusetts.
STATUS:	Abandoned, 1923.

LUBEC

ROUTE:	Eastport - Lubec	NUMBER:	141142
PORTS:	Eastport, Lubec, Way Ports	LENGTH:	69.5
COMPANY:	George A. Mowry, also	BREADTH:	18.0
	Passamaquoddy Ferry & Navigation Co.	DRAUGHT:	6.3
		GROSS TONNAGE:	50.0
BUILT:	1891 - J. H. Dyer, Portland, Maine.		
STATUS:	Crushed by ice at Winterport, Maine, 1941.		

Sumner T. Pike

EASTPORT

ROUTE: Eastport - Lubec
PORTS: Eastport, Lubec, Way Ports
COMPANY: Passamaquoddy Steam Ferry Co.
LOCATION: At North Lubec, Maine

BUILT: 1901 - Dennysville, Maine.
STATUS: Abandoned, 1939.

NUMBER:	136912
LENGTH:	76.0
BREADTH:	19.5
DRAUGHT:	6.5
GROSS TONNAGE:	64.0

Chapter 5

Mount Desert Island and Penobscot River Vessels

The steamers *T. F. SECOR* and *ROCKLAND* were operating in 1856.

The Coombs brothers of Belfast, Captain Perry and Captain Leighton, developed a colorful history while operating the steamers from Belfast to Castine.

Captain Oscar A. Crockett played an important part in developing the steamers running from Rockland to Eggemoggin Reach and Blue Hill. He later sold his fleet to the Eastern Steamship Company.

Captain I. E. Archibald of Rockland acquired an interesting history in building the line of steamers which ran from Rockland to Portland. He also sold to the Eastern Steamship Company.

An outstanding ship builder of this era was Samuel H. Barbour of Brewer. Eighteen of the steamers listed below were of his creation.

The forty-five vessels listed operated in this area: *T. F. SECOR, OLIVETTE, FRANCES, PERCY V., SORRENTO, SCHOODIC, E. T. SOMERS, FLORENCE, GOLDEN ROD, ISLESFORD, CREEDMOR* (small), *RUTH, MASCOT, ULYSSES, ROCKLAND, PENTAGOET, QUEEN CITY, CITY OF BANGOR* (small), *HENRY MORRISON, CIMBRIA, SEDGEWICK, VERONA, TREMONT* (small), *CREEDMOR* (large), *LITTLE BUTTERCUP, HECTOR, MINNEHAHA, SILVER STAR, ALICE HOWARD, MARJORIE, STOCKTON, CASTINE, ELECTA, CORINNA, ANNA BELLE, ISLESBORO, BLUE HILL, MARY MORGAN, ROCKLAND* (second), *GEORGE A. FULLER, W. G. BUTMAN, MAY ARCHER, SALACIA, GOVERNOR DOUGLAS, NEREID.*

T. F. SECOR

ROUTE:	Mount Desert - Penobscot	
PORTS:	Mount Desert, Penobscot Landings	
COMPANY:	Washington & Hancock Steam Navigation Co.	

NUMBER:	*
LENGTH:	135.0
BREADTH:	22.2
DRAUGHT:	17.5
GROSS TONNAGE:	228.0

BUILT: 1846 - New York, New York

HISTORY: First steamer to Mount Desert Island. Purchased by United States Government April 27, 1863, at New York.

STATUS: Burned while lying at Hilton Head, North Carolina, 1863.

* Official numbering did not begin until 1867.

OLIVETTE

ROUTE:	Plant Line	NUMBER:	155138
PORTS:	Boston, Bar Harbor	LENGTH:	274.3
COMPANY:	Plant Railroad & Steamship Co.	BREADTH:	35.2
		DRAUGHT:	11.6
		GROSS TONNAGE:	1611.0
		SPEED:	18 Knots

BUILT: 1887 - Wm. Cramp & Sons Co., Philadelphia, Pennsylvania.

HISTORY: In thick fog, running at full speed, she cut a small coastal schooner, loaded with ice, completely in half.

STATUS: Total loss on Cuban coast near Havana, January 12, 1918.

FRANCES

ROUTE:	Ports of Maine and Southern Nova Scotia	NUMBER:	9313
PORTS:	Bar Harbor in Summer, Bucksport in Winter,	LENGTH:	222.7
	and Digby, Nova Scotia via Milbridge,	BREADTH:	32.8
	Jonesport, Machias, Eastport	DRAUGHT:	10.0
COMPANY:	New England and Acadia Steamship Co.	GROSS TONNAGE:	988.18
BUILT:	1864 - Wilmington, Delaware.		

HISTORY: After several successful years Maine Central Railroad Co. obtained control. Home port changed to Rockland, Maine.

STATUS: Abandoned 1899.

F. E. Claes

PERCY V.

ROUTE:	Ellsworth - Swans Island	NUMBER:	150297
PORTS:	Ellsworth, Atlantic, Bass Harbor	LENGTH:	65.5
COMPANY:	Ellsworth, Blue Hill & Swans Island	BREADTH:	15.3
	Steamboat Co.	DRAUGHT:	5.8
OTHER NAME:	ANNA BELLE	GROSS TONNAGE:	37.2
LOCATION:	Ellsworth, Maine		
BUILT:	1883 - Bath, Maine		
HISTORY:	Built originally to run from Popham Beach to Bath for Fort Popham Summer Resident Association. Captain N. H. Sowle landed at Black's Island on notice. W. L. Remick was purser.		
STATUS:	Renamed ANNA BELLE. Abandoned 1924.		

SORRENTO

ROUTE:	Mount Desert Ferry - Sorrento -Bar Harbor	NUMBER:	126043
PORTS:	Mount Desert Ferry, Sorrento, Bar Harbor	LENGTH:	80.4
OTHER NAME:	*CITY POINT*	BREADTH:	17.5
LOCATION:	Docked at Steamboat Wharf,	DRAUGHT:	5.3
	Sorrento, Maine.	GROSS TONNAGE:	49.0
BUILT:	1882 - Boston, Massachusetts.		

HISTORY: Operated as *CITY POINT* in Boston, from 1882 until May 12, 1887. Ran in Frenchman's Bay, Maine, 1887 to 1893.

SCHOODIC

ROUTE:	Bar Harbor - Grindstone Neck	NUMBER:	204236
PORTS:	Bar Harbor, Winter Harbor	LENGTH:	85.0
COMPANY:	The Winter Harbor Transportation Co.	BREADTH:	20.6
LOCATION:	Grindstone Neck, Winter Harbor, Maine	DRAUGHT:	7.4
		GROSS TONNAGE:	11.0

BUILT: 1907 - Portland Co., Portland, Maine.

HISTORY: Ran from 1907 to 1924 in Frenchman's Bay, Maine. 1927-1935, Norfolk, Virginia.

STATUS: Burned, Feburary, 1947, at Drum Point, Patuxent River, Maryland.

E. T. SOMERS

ROUTE: Bar Harbor - Winter Harbor
PORTS: Bar Harbor, Winter Harbor
COMPANY: The Winter Harbor Transportation Co.

NUMBER:	218319
LENGTH:	76.8
BREADTH:	20.3
DRAUGHT:	6.4
GROSS TONNAGE:	64.0

BUILT: 1919 - White Haven, Maryland.

HISTORY: First home port was Reedville, Virginia. Second, Winter Harbor, Maine.

STATUS: Sold to Mexicans, 1934.

FLORENCE

ROUTE:	Mount Desert Island Stops		NUMBER:	120481
PORTS:	Cranberry Island, Southwest Harbor,		LENGTH:	78.4
	Way Landings		BREADTH:	17.8
COMPANY:	Captain Haddock		DRAUGHT:	4.6
			GROSS TONNAGE:	71.7
BUILT:	1882 - Barbour Brothers, Brewer, Maine.			
HISTORY:	In Maine Waters 1882 to 1904.			

GOLDEN ROD

ROUTE: Mount Desert Island Stops
PORTS: Bar Harbor, Southwest Harbor, Way Ports
COMPANY: A. Perry Coombs

NUMBER: 86250
LENGTH: 75.4
BREADTH: 15.2
DRAUGHT: 6.0
GROSS TONNAGE: 71.0

BUILT: 1893 - Barbour Brothers, Brewer, Maine.
HISTORY: Also serviced Penobscot River ports.
STATUS: Abandoned 1939. Hulk rests in Castine Harbor, Maine.

ISLESFORD

ROUTE: Mount Desert Island Stops

NUMBER:	100555
LENGTH:	49.4
BREADTH:	14.4
DRAUGHT:	5.2
GROSS TONNAGE:	27.0

BUILT: 1893 - S. H. Barbour, Brewer, Maine.
HISTORY: Also in Boothbay Harbor area, particularly the Damariscotta River Line.
STATUS: Abandoned 1941.

CREEDMOR (small)

NUMBER:	127322
LENGTH:	48.9
BREADTH:	12.9
DRAUGHT:	4.4
GROSS TONNAGE:	10.0

BUILT: 1899 - Barbour Brothers, Brewer, Maine.
HISTORY: Ran on Penobscot River.

RUTH

ROUTE: Bar Harbor - Bangor
PORTS: Bar Harbor, Bangor, Way Stops
COMPANY: The Brooksville and Bangor Steamboat Co.
OTHER NAME: *ATLANTIC*
NEAR
SISTER SHIP: *GOVERNOR BODWELL*
LOCATION: Entering Bar Harbor
BUILT: 1894 - Gilchrist's Yard, Rockland, Maine.
HISTORY: Renamed the *ATLANTIC*; registered in New York City, 1910. Registered at Washington, D.C., 1912-1916. Registered in Charleston, South Carolina, 1925.
STATUS: Foundered, September 10, 1925, in Cooper River, South Carolina.

NUMBER: 111059
LENGTH: 103.3
BREADTH: 23.7
DRAUGHT: 7.9
GROSS TONNAGE: 188.0

MASCOT

ROUTE:	Mount Desert Ferry	NUMBER:	92586
PORTS:	Bar Harbor, Mt. Desert Ferry	LENGTH:	63.0
COMPANY:	The Barbour Brothers Fleet	BREADTH:	15.5
LOCATION:	Sailing out of Bar Harbor, Maine	DRAUGHT:	6.0
		GROSS TONNAGE:	36.1

BUILT: 1894 - Barbour Brothers, Brewer, Maine.
STATUS: Abandoned, 1934.

W. H. Ballard

ULYSSES

ROUTE: Rockland - Bar Harbor
PORTS: Rockland, North Haven, Green's Landing
(Stonington), Southwest Harbor,
Bar Harbor, Hancock, Sullivan
COMPANY: The Rockland, Mount Desert & Sullivan Steamboat Co.
BUILT: 1864 - Mystic, Connecticut.
HISTORY: Ran for Nahant Steamboat Co. 1866 to 1876.
STATUS: January 10, 1878, wrecked beyond salvage at Rockland, Maine.

NUMBER: 25019
GROSS TONNAGE: 319.0

ROCKLAND

ROUTE:	Rockland - Mount Desert - Machias	NUMBER:	21175
PORTS:	Rockland, Machiasport, Way Ports	LENGTH:	134.3
COMPANY:	Rockland & Machias Steam	BREADTH:	21.6
	Navigation Co.	DRAUGHT:	7.3
		GROSS TONNAGE:	400.0
BUILT:	1853 - Hoboken, New Jersey.		
STATUS:	Sunk in Charleston Harbor, South Carolina, during Civil War.		

PENTAGOET

ROUTE:	New York - Rockland - Bangor	NUMBER:	150559
PORTS:	New York, Bangor, Way Ports	LENGTH:	128.8
COMPANY:	Manhattan Steamship Co.	BREADTH:	23.0
OTHER NAMES:	*HERO, MOCASSIN*	DRAUGHT:	16.7
		GROSS TONNAGE:	267.7

BUILT:	1864 - Philadelphia, Pennsylvania.
HISTORY:	Gun boat during Civil War.
STATUS:	Lost with all hands November 27, 1898. The steamer *PORTLAND* was lost in the same storm.

QUEEN CITY

ROUTE: Penobscot River
PORTS: Bangor, Rockland, Way Ports
COMPANY: Barbour Brothers
LOCATION: At a Bangor, Maine, Dock.

NUMBER: 20586
LENGTH: 92.4
BREADTH: 16.2
DRAUGHT: 5.6
GROSS TONNAGE: 115.72

BUILT: 1881 - Barbour Brothers, Brewer, Maine.
HISTORY: Sold 1887 to J. A. Petty of Providence, Rhode Island.
STATUS: Burned March 14, 1907, at Seaconnet Point, Rhode Island.

CITY OF BANGOR

ROUTE:	Bangor - Bar Harbor	NUMBER:	125726
PORTS:	Bangor, Bar Harbor, Way Ports	LENGTH:	104.3
COMPANY:	Bar Harbor Line	BREADTH:	19.9
OTHER NAME:	*CITY OF PORTSMOUTH*	DRAUGHT:	5.0
LOCATION:	At a Dock in Bangor, Maine.	GROSS TONNAGE:	159.3

BUILT: 1879 - Barbour Brothers, Brewer, Maine.

HISTORY: Renamed *CITY OF PORTSMOUTH*, May 27, 1883. Ran from Boston to Provincetown on South Shore Line 1882.

STATUS: Burned in Salem Harbor, Salem, Massachusetts, 1894.

HENRY MORRISON

ROUTE: Bangor - Bar Harbor
PORTS: Bangor, Bar Harbor, Way Ports
COMPANY: Oscar Crockett
OTHER NAMES: *BAR HARBOR, HENRY MORRISON*

NUMBER: 11129 (new off. #3396)
LENGTH: 120.0
BREADTH: 21.7
DRAUGHT: 7.2
GROSS TONNAGE: 259.9

BUILT: 1854 - Lawrence & Foulkes, Williamsburg, New York.

HISTORY: Lengthened and renamed *BAR HARBOR* by S. H. Barbour of Brewer, Maine, in 1888. He later renamed her the *HENRY MORRISON*.

STATUS: Burned at Winthrop, Massachusetts, April 6, 1898.

CIMBRIA

ROUTE:	Bangor - Bar Harbor	NUMBER:	126029
PORTS:	Bangor, Hampden, Winterport, Bucksport,	LENGTH:	116.7
	Sandy Point, Fort Point, Castine, Blake's	BREADTH:	30.0
	Point, Sargentville, Deer Isle, Sedgewick,	DRAUGHT:	7.6
	Bass Harbor, Southwest Harbor, Northeast,	GROSS TONNAGE:	275.0
	Harbor, Seal Harbor, Bar Harbor		
COMPANY:	The Barbour Line		
BUILT:	1882 - Barbour Brothers, Brewer, Maine.		
HISTORY:	Rebuilt 1899. Ran on Nahant Line in Boston Harbor 1906.		
STATUS:	Scrapped 1922 in Chicago, Illinois.		

SEDGEWICK

ROUTE: Penobscot River
PORTS: Bangor, Sandy Point, Castine, Islesboro, Hughes' Point, (Islesboro) Blake's Point, (Cape Rosier) Buck's Harbor (Brooksville).
COMPANY: Barbour Interests
OTHER NAMES: *GENERAL FRENCH, SEDGEWICK*
BUILT: 1892 - Barbour Brothers, Brewer, Maine.
HISTORY: Ran on Vinalhaven Run 1893. 1900 sold to the United States Government for use in Mobile, Alabama.
STATUS: Abandoned June 30, 1922.

NUMBER: 116499
LENGTH: 92.2
BREATH: 17.5
DRAUGHT: 6.4
GROSS TONNAGE: 155.5

VERONA

ROUTE:	Bangor - Bar Harbor - Way Ports	NUMBER:	161911
PORTS:	Bangor, Bar Harbor, Way Ports	LENGTH:	110.3
COMPANY:	Bangor & Bar Harbor Steamboat Co.	BREADTH:	28.0
		DRAUGHT:	8.0
		GROSS TONNAGE:	140.0
		SPEED:	14 Knots

BUILT: 1902 - Barbour Brothers, Brewer, Maine.

HISTORY: Ran excursions on Penobscot River. Sold to Connecticut group 1903.

STATUS: Burned November 27, 1907, at Highland Falls, New York.

TREMONT

ROUTE:	Penobscot River		NUMBER:	145689
PORTS:	Penobscot River Landings		LENGTH:	80.5
COMPANY:	Bangor & Bar Harbor Steamboat Co.		BREADTH:	21.6
LOCATION:	Docked at Bangor, Maine		DRAUGHT:	4.8
			GROSS TONNAGE:	81.0

BUILT: 1895 - Barbour Brotheres, Brewer, Maine, May 25.

STATUS: Abandoned near the Steamboat Wharf, Belfast, Maine, 1921.

CREEDMOR (large)

ROUTE:	Bar Harbor - Mount Desert Ferry	NUMBER:	126243
PORTS:	Bar Harbor, Hancock Point	LENGTH:	52.6
COMPANY:	Alfred E. Connors	BREADTH:	14.0
		DRAUGHT:	5.0
		GROSS TONNAGE:	19.43
BUILT:	1884 - Barbour Brothers, Brewer, Maine.		
STATUS:	Abandoned December 31, 1919.		

LITTLE BUTTERCUP

ROUTE:	Penobscot River - Frenchman's Bay	NUMBER:	140446
PORTS:	Bangor, Bar Harbor & Way Ports	LENGTH:	40.0
COMPANY:	Barbour Steamboat Company	BREADTH:	10.0
		DRAUGHT:	4.0
		GROSS TONNAGE:	14.89
BUILT:	1881 - Barbour Brothers, Brewer, Maine.		

HECTOR

ROUTE:	Penobscot River Service	NUMBER:	96217
PORTS:	Bangor, Rockland, Way Ports	LENGTH:	39.0
COMPANY:	Penobscot Steam Navigation Co.	BREADTH:	11.5
LOCATION:	At Bangor with Steamer *AWASHONKS* in Background	DRAUGHT:	4.2
		GROSS TONNAGE:	19.78

BUILT: 1893 - Bangor, Maine.

HISTORY: Also operated on the Bucksport - Castine Service, Union River Service, and Frenchman's Bay Service.

MINNEHAHA

ROUTE: Lamoine - Bar Harbor
PORTS: Lamoine, Bar Harbor
COMPANY: C. H. Knowlton
OTHER NAME: *MINNIE*

NUMBER: 91125
LENGTH: 50.6
BREADTH: 16.5
DRAUGHT: 4.1
GROSS TONNAGE: 18.0

BUILT: 1879 - Portland, Maine.
HISTORY: 1879-1888, Portland Harbor.
1888-1890, Lamoine - Bar Harbor.
1891-1914, Deer Isle, Maine.
Became *MINNIE* 1915.

SILVER STAR

ROUTE: Penobscot Bay
PORTS: Belfast, Castine, Brooksville

BUILT: 1886 - Barbour Brothers, Brewer, Maine.
STATUS: Abandoned 1923.

NUMBER: 116103
LENGTH: 73.5
BREADTH: 14.7
DRAUGHT: 4.8
GROSS TONNAGE: 75.0

ALICE HOWARD

ROUTE:	Belfast - Castine	NUMBER:	107464
PORTS:	Belfast, Castine	LENGTH:	73.1
COMPANY:	A. M. Devereux	BREADTH:	19.6
OTHER NAME:	*UTILITY*	DRAUGHT:	6.2

BUILT: 1899 - Peak's Island, Maine.

HISTORY: Renamed *UTILITY*, December 22, 1925, at Belfast, Maine.

STATUS: Sold to Cuba 1930.

MARJORIE

ROUTE:	Belfast - Brooklin	NUMBER:	92842
PORTS:	Belfast, Brooklin	LENGTH:	48.3
COMPANY:	The Barbour Line	BREADTH:	15.3
		DRAUGHT:	4.8
		GROSS TONNAGE:	29.0

BUILT:	1898 - Brewer, Maine.
HISTORY:	Ran from Bangor to West Brooksville.
STATUS:	Abandoned 1923 at Belfast, Maine.

STOCKTON

ROUTE:	Penobscot Bay	NUMBER:	91869
PORTS:	Bucksport, Verona Park, Sandy Point,	LENGTH:	81.5
	Belfast, Northport, Temple Heights,	BREADTH:	18.0
	Camden, Rockland	DRAUGHT:	5.6
COMPANY:	I. E. Archibald	GROSS TONNAGE:	98.0
OTHER NAMES:	*M & M, STOCKTON*		
BUILT:	1886 - Thomaston, Maine.		
STATUS:	Stripped at Rockland, Maine, 1905. Engine installed in new *MAY ARCHER*.		

CASTINE

ROUTE:	Castine Run, Islesboro Run, Rockland - Bangor Run	NUMBER:	126552
		LENGTH:	71.1
PORTS:	Penobscot River Ports	BREADTH:	14.5
COMPANY:	Coombs Brothers	DRAUGHT:	5.0
LOCATION:	Proceeding up the Penobscot River near the Waldo-Hancock Bridge.	GROSS TONNAGE:	69.0
BUILT:	1889 - Brewer, Maine.		
HISTORY:	Used also on charter work.		
STATUS:	Wrecked June 8, 1935, near Bay Ledges, Vinalhaven, Maine. Sixty-eight on board, three fatalities.		

ELECTA

ROUTE:	Frenchman's Bay	NUMBER:	135576
PORTS:	Sullivan, Bar Harbor	LENGTH:	64.0
COMPANY:	Frenchman's Bay Steamboat Line	BREADTH:	11.0
LOCATION:	Eastern Steamship Dock	DRAUGHT:	5.0
	Belfast, Maine	GROSS TONNAGE:	54.59
BUILT:	1882 - Brewer, Maine.		
HISTORY:	1882-1900 excursions from Belfast, Maine.		
	1910-1919 Boston Harbor excursions.		
STATUS:	Abandoned 1920.		

CORINNA

ROUTE:	Rockland - Castine	NUMBER:	127356
PORTS:	Rockland, Castine	LENGTH:	64.1
COMPANY:	Captain David Haskell	BREADTH:	15.6
		DRAUGHT:	6.2
		GROSS TONNAGE:	45.0

BUILT: 1899 - Portland, Maine.
HISTORY: Serviced Casco Bay for many years. Also ran on Kennebec River.
STATUS: Destroyed by fire at Brooksville, Maine, September 12, 1915.

ANNA BELLE

ROUTE:	Penobscot Bay Ports		NUMBER:	150297
OTHER NAME:	*PERCY V.*		LENGTH:	65.5
LOCATION:	Warren's Landing, Islesboro, Maine		BREADTH:	15.3
			DRAUGHT:	5.8
			GROSS TONNAGE:	37.21

BUILT:	1883 - Bath, Maine.
HISTORY:	Renamed *ANNA BELLE* 1909.
STATUS:	Abandoned 1924.

ISLESBORO

ROUTE:	Camden - Islesboro - Belfast	NUMBER:	212877
PORTS:	Camden, Islesboro, Belfast	LENGTH:	74.5
OTHER NAMES:	*U.S.S. ISLESBORO, CITY OF SOUTHPORT*	BREADTH:	18.0
		DRAUGHT:	6.8
		GROSS TONNAGE:	119.0

BUILT: 1914 - Cobb-Butler Yard, Rockland, Maine.

HISTORY: United States Navy during World War I. Renamed *CITY OF SOUTHPORT* 1927 at Baltimore. Operated as motorized freight boat 1942. Owned by Martin Fish Co., Inc., Crisfield, Maryland, 1965.

BLUE HILL

ROUTE:	Rockland - Blue Hill - Ellsworth Line		NUMBER:	3384
PORTS:	Rockland, Blue Hill, Ellsworth,		LENGTH:	135.0
	Way Ports		BREADTH:	18.0
COMPANY:	The Rockland & Ellsworth Steamboat Co.		DRAUGHT:	7.0
			GROSS TONNAGE:	187.31

BUILT: 1887 - William McKie, East Boston, Massachusetts.
HISTORY: Sold in Canada, 1889. Yarmouth & Shelburne Steamship Co., 1891.
            Sold to Bras D'Or Steamship Co., 1893.

MARY MORGAN

ROUTE: Bangor - Rockland
PORTS: Penobscot River Ports
COMPANY: Charles Morgan
OTHER NAMES: *ANGLER, W. L. DAVIS, E. MADISON HALL*

NUMBER: 91079
LENGTH: 166.5
BREADTH: 28.0
DRAUGHT: 8.0
GROSS TONNAGE: 409.0

BUILT: 1878 - Wilmington, Delaware
HISTORY: 1887 - ran from Bangor to Rockland as *MARY MORGAN*.
1888 - returned to Wilmington, Delaware. Renamed *ANGLER*. Later named *E. MADISON HALL*.

ROCKLAND (2)

ROUTE:	Penobscot River		NUMBER:	110581
PORTS:	Penobscot River, Way Ports		LENGTH:	98.9
COMPANY:	Boston & Bangor Steamship Co.		BREADTH:	16.5
OTHER NAME:	*INTERSTATE PARK*		DRAUGHT:	6.7
			GROSSTONNAGE:	135.0

BUILT: 1883 - Boston, Massachusetts.

HISTORY: Built from leftover material obtained from the construction of *S.S. PENOBSCOT*. Renamed *INTERSTATE PARK* at New York, 1915.

STATUS: Abandoned 1926.

GEORGE A. FULLER

ROUTE:	Stonington - Deer Isle Quarry
PORTS:	Stonington Harbor
COMPANY:	Deer Isle Granite Co.
OTHER NAMES:	*SHETUCKET, DORIS*
LOCATION:	Eastern Steamship Dock at Stonington, Maine
BUILT:	1912 - Noank, Connecticut
HISTORY:	1913 - New London, Connecticut.
	1915-1917 - Gloucester, Massachusetts.
	1918-1922 - Portsmouth, New Hampshire.
	1923 - Stonington, Maine.
	1925 - New York City.

NUMBER:	209869
LENGTH:	56.6
BREADTH:	18.0
DRAUGHT:	5.0
GROSS TONNAGE:	14.0

W. G. BUTMAN

ROUTE:	Rockland - Matinicus - Criehaven		NUMBER:	81542
PORTS:	Rockland, Matinicus, Criehaven		LENGTH:	64.2
			BREADTH:	15.4
			DRAUGHT:	5.9
			GROSS TONNAGE:	43.0

BUILT: 1896 - East Boothbay, Maine

STATUS: May 26, 1915, foundered in West Penobscot Bay, Maine. Passengers rescued.

MAY ARCHER

ROUTE:	Boothbay - Monhegan - Thomaston	NUMBER:	20319
PORTS:	Boothbay, Monhegan, Thomaston	LENGTH:	80.
COMPANY:	I. E. Archibald	BREADTH:	20
LOCATION:	Monhegan Island, Maine	DRAUGHT:	7.
		GROSS TONNAGE:	125

BUILT: 1906 - Rockland, Maine, Cobb-Butler Yard.

HISTORY: Ran Winters around Mount Desert Island. Ran from Isles of Shoals 1913. Was employed for a whi in Boston. Later on BLock Island - Providence - Newport Run.

STATUS: Totally destroyed by fire, May 20, 1934, at Quincy, Massachusetts.

SALACIA

ROUTE:	Portland - Boothbay Harbor	NUMBER:	116683
PORTS:	Portland, Boothbay, Way Ports	LENGTH:	120.9
COMPANY:	The Maine Coast Navigation Co.	BREADTH:	26.2
OTHER NAME:	*NORFOLK-ON-THE-ROADS*	DRAUGHT:	10.0
		GROSS TONNAGE:	332.4

BUILT: 1895 - Bath, Maine.

HISTORY: Sailed from New York, January 4, 1899, to Puerto Rico.
Renamed *NORFOLK-ON-THE-ROADS* 1900.
Rebuilt 1902 after a fire at Norfolk, Virginia. Used by Norfolk & Atlantic Terminal Co.

GOVERNOR DOUGLAS

ROUTE:	Boothbay - Monhegan - Thomaston	NUMBER:	136819
PORTS:	Boothbay, Monhegan, Thomaston	LENGTH:	56.6
COMPANY:	Captain I. E. Archibald of Rockland, Maine	BREADTH:	16.4
OTHER NAME:	*EMPRESS*	DRAUGHT:	6.4
		GROSS TONNAGE:	35.0

BUILT:	1900 - Essex, Massachusetts.
HISTORY:	First gasoline operated 1900-1910.
	Later operated steam 1911-1926.
	Eventually became diesel 1927-1935.
STATUS:	Burned December 31, 1935, Portland, Maine. Two lives lost.

NEREID

ROUTE:	Boothbay - Monhegan - Thomaston	NUMBER:	231625
PORTS:	Boothbay, Monhegan, Thomaston	LENGTH:	60.8
LOCATION:	Entering Monhegan Island, Maine	BREADTH:	15.7
		DRAUGHT:	8.2
		GROSS TONNAGE:	46.0
BUILT:	1923 - Thomaston, Maine.		

Chapter 6

Kennebec and Boothbay Vessels

Following the Civil War the Kennebec area was provided with regular service from Boston to Bath and Gardiner. The vessels used are shown in Chapter IF, Kennebec Line.

Several other vessels on the Kennebec and in the Boothbay service were: *CITY OF WATERVILLE, DELLA COLLINS* (later Eastern), *LIZZIE M. SNOW, SASANDA, ISLANDER, ISLANDER* (2), *VIRGINIA, GARDINER, TOURIST, ANODYNE, BRISTOL, NEWCASTLE, WINTER HARBOR, NELLIE G., NELLIE G. II, NORMAN II, JULE* and *ELDORADO.*

This area has always been one of the most popular on the Maine coast for summer residents.

CITY OF WATERVILLE

ROUTE:	Waterville, Augusta, Maine	NUMBER:	126637
	via the Lock at Augusta	LENGTH:	74.6
PORTS:	Waterville, Augusta	BREADTH:	19.9
		DRAUGHT:	3.6
		GROSS TONNAGE:	36.6

BUILT: 1890 - Barbour Brothers, Brewer, Maine.

HISTORY: Sold, July, 1896, at Baltimore for excursion trade between Point Breeze and Locust Point, Maryland.

STATUS: Abandoned, 1903.

R. B. Sanborn

DELLA COLLINS

ROUTE:	Kennebec River	NUMBER:	6973
PORTS:	Augusta, Hallowell, Gardiner	LENGTH:	106.8
COMPANY:	Jason Collins	BREADTH:	20.6
LOCATION:	Passing through the only covered drawbridge	DRAUGHT:	5.3
	in Maine, connecting Gardiner and Randolph.	GROSS TONNAGE:	194.0
BUILT:	1879 - East Boston, Massachusetts.		
HISTORY:	This stern wheeler owned by Eastern Steamship Company in later years.		
STATUS:	Junked 1907 at Ocean Point on the Kennebec River in Maine.		

F. E. Claes

LIZZIE M. SNOW

ROUTE: Augusta - Bath
PORTS: Augusta, Bath
COMPANY: The Augusta & Bath Steamboat Co.

BUILT: 1889 - Barbour Brothers, Brewer, Maine.
STATUS: Abandoned 1903.

NUMBER: 141012
LENGTH: 35.7
BREADTH: 9.9
DRAUGHT: 3.9
GROSS TONNAGE: 17.13

R. B. Sanborn

SASANDA

ROUTE:	Kennebec River Service	NUMBER:	23866
PORTS:	Bath, Boothbay, Way Ports	LENGTH:	81.3
COMPANY:	Eastern Steamboat Co., Bath, Maine	BREADTH:	15.3
OTHER NAME:	*ANNIE AND MAGGIE*	DRAUGHT:	7.0
		GROSS TONNAGE:	59.72

BUILT: 1870 - Bath, Maine

HISTORY: Sold to a Staten Island, New York, company, 1887.
            Renamed *ANNIE AND MAGGIE*, June 9, 1890, at New York.

STATUS: Abandoned 1900.

J. T. Beck

ISLANDER

ROUTE:	Kennebec River - Boothbay Harbor	NUMBER:	100328
PORTS:	Kennebec River, Boothbay Region Stops	LENGTH:	106.2
		BREADTH:	19.0
		DRAUGHT:	6.8
		GROSS TONNAGE:	119.0
		SPEED:	15 Knots

BUILT: 1883 - Bath, Maine.

HISTORY: Sold 1900 to Sakonet Transportation Co. of Providence, Rhode Island. At a later date ran in New York Harbor.

STATUS: Burned June 2, 1926, at Southport, North Carolina.

ISLANDER (2)

ROUTE:	Kennebec River - Boothbay Harbor	NUMBER:	20500
PORTS:	Kennebec River, Boothbay Harbor Region Stops	LENGTH:	80.
COMPANY:	Augusta, Gardiner, Boothbay Steamboat Co.	BREADTH:	19.
LOCATION:	Boothbay Harbor, Maine	DRAUGHT:	6.
		GROSS TONNAGE:	75.

BUILT: 1908 - W. I. Adams & Co. Shipyard, East Boothbay, Maine.
HISTORY: Sold 1926 to Circle Line for New York Harbor Service.

VIRGINIA

ROUTE:	Bath - Boothbay Harbor Service	NUMBER:	206364
PORTS:	Bath, MacMahan, Five Islands, Southport,	LENGTH:	66.3
	Capital Island, Squirrel Island, Boothbay Harbor	BREADTH:	18.5
LOCATION:	Off the Dock at Bath, Maine	DRAUGHT:	6.3
		GROSS TONNAGE:	71.0
BUILT:	1909 - Bath, Maine.		
HISTORY:	Built to replace ELDORADO.		
STATUS:	Ran 1940. Burned 1944 at Boothbay, Maine.		

GARDINER

ROUTE:	Kennebec River - Boothbay Ports	NUMBER:	8625
PORTS:	Kennebec River, Boothbay Stops	LENGTH:	65.
COMPANY:	Augusta & Bath Steamboat Co.	BREADTH:	14.
		DRAUGHT:	5.
		GROSS TONNAGE:	38.

BUILT:	1893 - Bath, Maine.
HISTORY:	Sold to New York interests 1910.
STATUS:	Abandoned 1917.

TOURIST

ROUTE:	Damariscotta River	NUMBER:	205213
PORTS:	Damariscotta, South Bristol, Christmas Cove,	LENGTH:	45.2
	Pemaquid, Boothbay Harbor	BREADTH:	15.3
COMPANY:	Damariscotta Steamboat Co.	DRAUGHT:	5.4
OTHER NAME:	*SABINO*	GROSS TONNAGE:	24.0
LOCATION:	Entering Damariscotta, Maine	SPEED:	8 Knots
BUILT:	1908 - East Boothbay, Maine.		
HISTORY:	Popham Beach Steamboat Co., 1921-1927.		
	Casco Bay Line and Captain H. P. Williams, 1927-1961.		
	Philip Corbin, 1961-1972.		
	Maritime Museum,. Mystic, Connecticut, 1972.		

ANODYNE

ROUTE:	Damariscotta River	NUMBER:	107163
PORTS:	Damariscotta, River Ports, Boothbay	LENGTH:	36.0
COMPANY:	Damariscotta River Steamboat Co.	BREADTH:	9.9
LOCATION:	Damariscotta, Maine	DRAUGHT:	4.3
		GROSS TONNAGE:	13.0

BUILT: 1895 - Bristol, Maine.

HISTORY: Built to advertise and sell Johnson's Anodyne Liniment. Later rebuilt for Damariscotta River Service.

STATUS: Removed from registry, 1922; sold to Canadian parties.

Harold W. Castner

BRISTOL

ROUTE:	Damariscotta - Boothbay	NUMBER:	3879
PORTS:	Damariscotta, Boothbay	LENGTH:	67.9
COMPANY:	Damariscotta River Steamboat Co.	BREADTH:	16.9
LOCATION:	Damariscotta, Maine	DRAUGHT:	6.2
		GROSS TONNAGE:	48.0

BUILT:	1901 - Bristol, Maine.
HISTORY:	Sold in New York, 1909.
STATUS:	Burned November 26, 1919, Mariner's Harbor, New York.

Harold W. Castner

NEWCASTLE

ROUTE:	Damariscotta - Boothbay	NUMBER:	130963
PORTS:	Damariscotta, Boothbay, Way Ports	LENGTH:	80.0
COMPANY:	Damariscotta River Steamboat Co.	BREADTH:	17.9
OTHER NAME:	*PELHAM*	DRAUGHT:	6.9
LOCATION:	Damariscotta, Maine	GROSS TONNAGE:	83.0
BUILT:	1902 - Bristol, Maine.		
HISTORY:	1928 sold at public auction to Oakland Beach - Long Island Ferry Service.		
STATUS:	In service 1936.		

WINTER HARBOR

ROUTE:	Wiscasset Run	NUMBER:	81162
PORTS:	Transfer boat between Boothbay, Linekin Bay,	LENGTH:	70.4
	South Bristol, Pemaquid Harbor, Wiscasset	BREADTH:	14.0
COMPANY:	Eastern Steamboat Co.	DRAUGHT:	4.5
		GROSS TONNAGE:	36.0

BUILT: 1887 - New England Shipbuilding Co., Bath, Maine.

HISTORY: Built to run from Mount Desert Island to Winter Harbor, Maine. Wiscasset - Boothbay route, 1908 to 1932.

STATUS: Sunk at Wiscasset, Maine, November 14, 1932.

Chester Swett

NELLIE G.

ROUTE: Falmouth Foreside, Maine - Cousins, Little John and Chebeague Islands

PORTS: Falmouth Foreside, Cousins, Little John, Chebeague Islands

COMPANY: Falmouth Foreside Development Co.

LOCATION: Boothbay Harbor, Maine

BUILT: 1895 - Woolwich, Maine.

HISTORY: Ferry between Boothbay Harbor and Squirrel Island, Maine, 1895-1932. Casco Bay, 1933-1951. Changd from steam to motor, 1933.

STATUS: Burned at Casco Bay, Maine, 1951.

NUMBER: 130692
LENGTH: 36.8
BREADTH: 10.3
DRAUGHT: 3.5
GROSS TONNAGE: 9.0

NELLIE G. II

ROUTE:	Boothbay - Squirrel Island	NUMBER:	1-C59
PORTS:	Boothbay, Squirrel Island	LENGTH:	44.0
COMPANY:	Captain Ross Dickson	BREADTH:	11.0
LOCATION:	Boothbay Harbor, Maine	DRAUGHT:	3.5
		GROSS TONNAGE:	11.0

BUILT: 1936 - East Boothbay, Maine.

James Stevens

NORMAN II

ROUTE: Bath - Boothbay Harbor Service
PORTS: Bath, MacMahan, Five Islands, Southport,
     Capital Island, Squirrel Island, Boothbay
LOCATION: Boothbay Harbor, Maine

BUILT: 1911 - Wiscasset, Maine.

NUMBER: 208597
LENGTH: 44.5
BREADTH: 12.5
DRAUGHT: 5.3
GROSS TONNAGE: 16.0

James Stevens

JULE

ROUTE:	Bath - Boothbay Harbor Service	NUMBER:	77364
PORTS:	Bath, Boothbay, Way Ports	LENGTH:	50.7
COMPANY:	Celia C. Etheridge	BREADTH:	12.3
LOCATION:	Boothbay Harbor, Maine	DRAUGHT:	4.5
		GROSS TONNAGE:	14.0

BUILT: 1899 - Weymouth, Massachusetts.

HISTORY: 1900-1909 Boston, Massachusetts.
            1910-1914 Damariscotta, Maine.
            1915-1924 Rockland, Maine.
            1925-1926 Portland, Maine.
            1927-1939 Bristol, Maine.

STATUS: Abandoned 1941.

W. H. Ballard

ELDORADO

ROUTE: Bath - Popham Beach Line
PORTS: Bath, Popham Beach
COMPANY: Popham Beach Steamboat Co.
LOCATION: Popham Beach, Maine

BUILT: 1893 - Buffalo, New York.
HISTORY: In Maine 1896 to 1908.
STATUS: Burned December 16, 1908, Phippsburg, Maine.

NUMBER: 136349
LENGTH: 73.2
BREADTH: 17.0
DRAUGHT: 6.4
GROSS TONNAGE: 96.0

Chapter 7

Casco Bay Vessels

Twenty-six vessels serving this area were: *ENTERPRISE, GORDON, ALICE, PRISCILLA, CADET, GREENWOOD, PHANTOM, MADELEINE, CHEBEAGUE, FOREST CITY, PEJEPSCOT, LOUISE, COMET, ADMIRAL, SABINO, GURNET, TOURIST, EMITA, MAQUOIT, FOREST QUEEN, SEBASCODEGAN, MERRYCONEAG, AUCOCISCO, PILGRIM, MACHIGONNE* and *S. E. SPRING.* The *CADET* operated as early as 1880. Included is a map of the Casco Bay area.

Three paddle-wheel steamboats operated in Portland Harbor: *FOREST CITY* in this chapter; also *S. E. SPRING*, which ran from Portland to Old Orchard; *SWAMPSCOTT*, in Chapter 9, a ferry boat originally running in Boston Harbor, but later from Portland to Peake's Island. Predecessors of Casco Bay Lines date to the 1880's. Casco Bay and Harpswell Company, formed in 1907, went bankrupt in 1919. Casco Bay Lines, incorporated in 1920, maintains the service today.

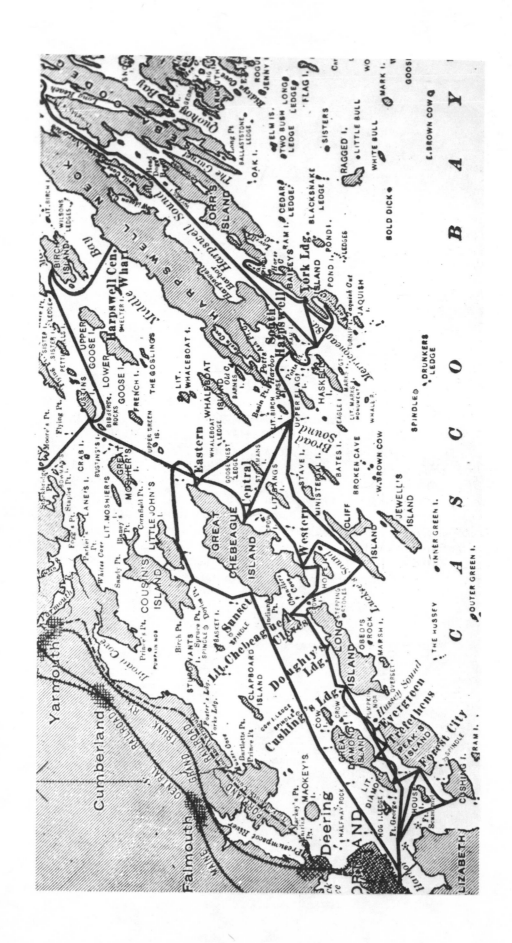

Chester Swett

ENTERPRISE

ROUTE: Portland - Boothbay
PORTS: Portland, Casco Bay, Boothbay Stops
COMPANY: Eastern Steamship Corp.
LOCATION: East Boothbay (Maine) Pier

BUILT: 1882 - Wilmington, Delaware.
HISTORY: In Maine from 1890 to 1913.
STATUS: Not listed after 1914.

NUMBER: 135619
LENGTH: 118.0
BREADTH: 22.0
DRAUGHT: 7.0
GROSS TONNAGE: 183.0

GORDON

ROUTE:	Casco Bay	NUMBER:	115469
PORTS:	Portland, Harpswell	LENGTH:	71.8
COMPANY:	Harpswell Steamboat Co.	BREADTH:	15.8
OTHER NAME:	*SEA FLOWER*	DRAUGHT:	5.0
		GROSS TONNAGE:	45.07

BUILT:	1876 - Clark's Island, Maine.
HISTORY:	Ran with *ALICE*, 1886, Harpswell Steamboat Company.
STATUS:	Not listed after 1890.

Paul D. Tapley

ALICE

ROUTE: Casco Bay

PORTS: Portland, Long Island, Little Chebeague,
                Jenks, Harpswell, Orr's Island

COMPANY: Harpswell Steamboat Co.

BUILT: 1884 - Brewer, Maine.

HISTORY: Portland, Maine 1884-1898.
                Eastport, Maine 1899-1904.

STATUS: Not listed after 1905.

NUMBER:	106277
LENGTH:	53.2
BREADTH:	14.1
DRAUGHT:	4.3
GROSS TONNAGE:	12.14

F. E. Claes

PRISCILLA

ROUTE: Casco Bay
PORTS: Casco Bay Ports

BUILT: 1901 - Essex, Massachusetts.

NUMBER: 150905
LENGTH: 62.8
BREADTH: 17.4
DRAUGHT: 8.2
GROSS TONNAGE: 67.0

CADET

ROUTE: Casco Bay
PORTS: Casco Bay Ports
COMPANY: Casco Bay Steamboat Co.

BUILT: 1879 - Newburgh, New York.
STATUS: Dropped from registry 1897.

NUMBER: 12528
LENGTH: 88.6
BREADTH: 16.6
DRAUGHT: 6.0
GROSS TONNAGE: 65.63

GREENWOOD

ROUTE:	Casco Bay	NUMBER:	85962
PORTS:	Casco Bay Ports	LENGTH:	56.2
		BREADTH:	16.0
		DRAUGHT:	6.0
		GROSS TONNAGE:	28.79

BUILT: 1887 - Portland, Maine.
HISTORY: 1887-1892 Casco Bay.
            1893 - (Eastport - Lubec - Campobello) Eastport, Maine.
STATUS: Disappeared from MVUS without explanation 1894.

PHANTOM

ROUTE: Casco Bay - Portland Harbor
PORTS: Casco Bay Ports
COMPANY: Freeport Steamboat Co.
LOCATION: Portland Dock

BUILT: 1887 - South Freeport, Maine.
HISTORY: Portland 1887-1898.
Eastport 1900-1909.

NUMBER: 150414
LENGTH: 65.0
BREADTH: 15.3
DRAUGHT: 6.1
GROSS TONNAGE: 38.28

The Peabody Museum of Salem

MADELEINE

ROUTE:	Casco Bay	NUMBER:	92523
PORTS:	Portland, Great Diamond Island,	LENGTH:	86.0
	Mackworths, Falmouth Foreside	BREADTH:	18.6
COMPANY:	Falmouth Foreside Steamboat Co.	DRAUGHT:	6.7
LOCATION:	A Portland Pier	GROSS TONNAGE:	70.36
BUILT:	1893 - Cape Elizabeth, Maine.		
STATUS:	Abandoned, January 10, 1912, twelve miles southeast of Cape Lookout Light Ship, North Carolina. No lives lost.		

CHEBEAGUE

ROUTE:	Casco Bay		NUMBER:	126716
PORTS:	Casco Bay Ports		LENGTH:	71.7
COMPANY:	Harpswell Steamboat Co.		BREADTH:	17.0
			DRAUGHT:	6.6
			GROSS TONNAGE:	47.67

BUILT: 1891 - Portland, Maine.

HISTORY: *ENGINE #7*, Portland Fire Department, Portland,

STATUS: Not listed after 1898.

FOREST CITY

ROUTE:	Casco Bay	NUMBER:	10609
PORTS:	Casco Bay Ports	LENGTH:	117.8
COMPANY:	The Forest City Steamboat Co.	BREADTH:	18.6
OTHER NAME:	*GAZELLE*	DRAUGHT:	6.6
		GROSS TONNAGE:	247.24

BUILT:	1865 - Portland, Maine.
HISTORY:	Renamed *FOREST CITY*, May 8, 1884.
STATUS:	Broken up Baltimore, Maryland, September 11, 1902.

Frank Claes

PEJEPSCOT

ROUTE: Casco Bay
PORTS: Casco Bay Ports
COMPANY: McDonald Steamboat Co.
OTHER NAME: *SEA GATE*
LOCATION: Gurnet, Maine
BUILT: 1894 - Newburgh, New York.
HISTORY: Portland, Maine, 1901-1902. New York, 1903-1923.
STATUS: Abandoned 1923.

NUMBER: 150818
LENGTH: 97.0
BREADTH: 20.1
DRAUGHT: 5.8
GROSS TONNAGE: 125.0

W. H. Ballard

LOUISE

ROUTE: Presumpscot River - Portland Harbor
PORTS: Portland Harbor
COMPANY: Presumpscot River Steamboat Co.

BUILT: 1885 - South Portland, Maine.
HISTORY: Abandoned 1896.

NUMBER: 141377
LENGTH: 59.5
BREADTH: 15.2
DRAUGHT: 4.5
GROSS TONNAGE: 27.5

T. H. Franklin

COMET

ROUTE:	Portland - West Bath, Maine		NUMBER:	127563
PORTS:	Portland, New Meadows Inn		LENGTH:	54.6
			BREADTH:	17.3
			DRAUGHT:	6.1
			GROSS TONNAGE:	77.0

BUILT: 1901 - Portland, Maine.
STATUS: Foundered May 26, 1939, Arlington, Staten Island, New York.

ADMIRAL

ROUTE:	Casco Bay	NUMBER:	22203
PORTS:	Casco Bay Ports	LENGTH:	38.0
COMPANY:	Casco Bay Lines	BREADTH:	13.6
LOCATION:	Casco Bay Lines' Wharf, Portland, Maine	DRAUGHT:	4.0
		GROSS TONNAGE:	70.0
BUILT:	1906 - Camden, New Jersey.		
STATUS:	Dismantled, Portland, Maine, 1954.		

SABINO

ROUTE:	Casco Bay	NUMBER:	205213
PORTS:	Casco Bay Ports	LENGTH:	45.2
COMPANY:	Casco Bay Lines	BREADTH:	15.3
OTHER NAME:	*TOURIST*	DRAUGHT:	5.4
LOCATION:	Casco Bay Lines' Pier, Portland, Maine	GROSS TONNAGE:	24.0
		SPEED:	8 Knots

BUILT: 1908 - East Boothbay, Maine.

HISTORY: 1908-1921 Damariscotta Steamboat Co.
1921-1927 Popham Beach Steamboat Co.
1927-1961 H. P. Williams and/or Casco Bay Lines.
1961 Philip Corbin.

STATUS: 1979 - Mystic Seaport, making daily trips on Mystic River, Connecticut.

J. T. Beck

GURNET

ROUTE:	Casco Bay	NUMBER:	212259
PORTS:	Casco Bay Ports	LENGTH:	58.6
COMPANY:	Casco Bay Lines	BREADTH:	18.0
LOCATION:	Portland Harbor, Maine	DRAUGHT:	6.2
		GROSS TONNAGE:	70.0
BUILT:	1914 - Boothbay Harbor, Maine.		
STATUS:	Abandoned 1947.		

J. T. Beck

TOURIST (2)

ROUTE:	Casco Bay	NUMBER:	211673
PORTS:	Casco Bay Ports	LENGTH:	58.4
COMPANY:	Casco Bay Lines	BREADTH:	16.2
LOCATION:	Tied up in Portland Harbor, Maine	DRAUGHT:	5.6
		GROSS TONNAGE:	33.0

BUILT: 1913 - Boothbay Harbor, Maine.
STATUS: Burned for scrap, March 19, 1955.

W. H. Ballard

EMITA

ROUTE:	Portland - Casco Bay	NUMBER:	135431
PORTS:	Casco Bay Ports	LENGTH:	84.0
COMPANY:	Casco Bay Lines	BREADTH:	23.6
LOCATION:	Portland Harbor, Maine	DRAUGHT:	5.9
		GROSS TONNAGE:	111.0

BUILT: 1880 - For Catskill Lines at Athens, New York.

HISTORY: Used excursions Portland to Old Orchard, August, 1883.
Used on Greenwood Garden Line, June, 1886.
Franklin Wharf, Portland, to Peaks Island, Cushing Island and Cape Cottage.
Captain Roscoe Kent, Swans Island, Maine, was one of her last captains.

STATUS: Abandoned 1956.

MAQUOIT

ROUTE: Portland - Casco Bay
PORTS: Casco Bay Ports
COMPANY: Casco Bay Lines

BUILT: 1904 - South Portland, Maine.
STATUS: Abandoned September, 1951.

NUMBER:	200852
LENGTH:	85.0
BREADTH:	20.5
DRAUGHT:	7.6
GROSS TONNAGE:	108.0

FOREST QUEEN

ROUTE: Portland - Casco Bay
PORTS: Casco Bay Ports
COMPANY: Casco Bay Steamboat Co.
LOCATION: At Portland dock

BUILT: 1887 - Athens, New York.
STATUS: Sold to Cuban owners, 1930.

NUMBER: 129689
LENGTH: 100.8
BREADTH: 22.2
DRAUGHT: 8.9
GROSS TONNAGE: 138.9

SEBASCODEGAN

ROUTE:	Portland - Casco Bay	NUMBER:	116671
PORTS:	Casco Bay Ports	LENGTH:	103.8
COMPANY:	Casco Bay Lines	BREADTH:	24.8
OTHER NAME:	*COMMANDER*	DRAUGHT:	8.9
		GROSS TONNAGE:	160.7
BUILT:	1895 - South Portland, Maine.		
STATUS:	Abandoned, 1930.		

Deer Isle - Stonington Historical Society

MERRYCONEAG

ROUTE:	Portland - Casco Bay	NUMBER:	92012
PORTS:	Casco Bay Ports	LENGTH:	95.8
COMPANY:	Casco Bay Lines	BREADTH:	22.5
		DRAUGHT:	8.9
		GROSS TONNAGE:	165.0

BUILT: 1888 - East Deering, Maine.

HISTORY: Portland - Casco Bay, 1888-1892.
                 Portland - Rockland, 1893-1905.
                 Penobscot River, 1906.
                 Casco Bay, 1907-1918.

STATUS: Burned to water's edge at Orr's Island, Maine, November 29, 1918.

AUCOCISCO

ROUTE:	Portland - Casco Bay		NUMBER:	107286
PORTS:	Casco Bay Ports		LENGTH:	107.8
COMPANY:	Casco Bay Lines		BREADTH:	24.9
			DRAUGHT:	8.9
			GROSS TONNAGE:	167.0

BUILT: 1897 - South Portland, Maine.
HISTORY: Originally built for Harpswell Steamboat Co.
STATUS: Dismantled 1953, Portland, Maine.

W. H. Ballard

PILGRIM

ROUTE:	Portland - Casco Bay	NUMBER:	150524
PORTS:	Casco Bay Ports	LENGTH:	113.7
COMPANY:	Casco Bay Lines	BREADTH:	26.0
		DRAUGHT:	7.9
		GROSS TONNAGE:	261.0

BUILT: 1891 - Buffalo, New York.
HISTORY: Statue of Liberty Boat, 1936.
STATUS: Burned March 27, 1937, Bayonne, New Jersey.

R. Loren Graham

MACHIGONNE

ROUTE: Portland - Casco Bay
PORTS: Casco Bay Ports
COMPANY: Casco Bay Lines
OTHER NAMES: *HOOK MT., BLOCK ISLAND (2), LEAGUE ISLAND, YANKEE*
LOCATION: Casco Bay
BUILT: 1907 - Neafie & Levy, Philadelphia, Pennsylvania.
STATUS: See *BLOCK ISLAND (2)*, also *YANKEE*.

NUMBER: 203969
LENGTH: 126.5
BREADTH: 29.0
DRAUGHT: 9.6
GROSS TONNAGE: 425.0
SPEED: 12 Knots

S. E. SPRING

ROUTE:	Portland - Old Orchard	NUMBER:	115776
PORTS:	Portland, East Deering,	LENGTH:	93.7
	Biddeford Pool, Old Orchard, Maine	BREADTH:	19.0
COMPANY:	Old Orchard Steamboat Co.	DRAUGHT:	4.8
		GROSS TONNAGE:	154.0

BUILT: 1881 - East Deering, Maine. Machinery built by Portland Co.

HISTORY: 1889-1894, Salem Willows and Baker's Island, Massachusetts.
1901, sold to New York parties. Sailed between New York City and City Island.

Chapter 8

North of Boston Vessels

The steamers *PIONEER, VIKING* and *SIGHTSEER* operated from Portsmouth, New Hampshire to the Isles of Shoals, *CITY OF PORTSMOUTH* from Boston to the Isles of Shoals and to Portsmouth, and *BALTIMORE* ran the same route.

The stern-wheeler *MERRIMAC* operated on the Merrimack River between Haverhill and Newburyport, making several way landings. *CITY OF HAVERHILL* ran from Haverhill to Boston and made stops en route to Gloucester. The Boston and Gloucester Steamboat Company operated *CITY OF GLOUCESTER*, the new *CAPE ANN* and finally *MASCOT*.

The Nahant Steamboat Company operated a number of ships between Boston and Nahant. Shown are: *NELLY BAKER, ADELAIDE, NAHANT, WINTHROP* and *NASSAU*.

PIONEER

ROUTE: The Isles of Shoals

PORTS: Portsmouth, New Hampshire, Isles of Shoals

COMPANY: Concord & Portsmouth Railway Co.

NUMBER: 1999

LENGTH: 92.

BREADTH: 31.

DRAUGHT: 5.

GROSS TONNAGE: 103.1

BUILT: 1864 - Portsmouth, New Hampshire.

HISTORY: Portsmouth - Isles of Shoals 1864.
               Rockland - Vinalhaven, Maine 1869.

STATUS: Foundered November 23, 1915, Barnstable Light, Massachusetts. Three on board, no lives los

CITY OF PORTSMOUTH

ROUTE:	Boston - Portsmouth, New Hampshire	NUMBER:	125726
PORTS:	Boston, Isles of Shoals, Portsmouth	LENGTH:	104.3
OTHER NAME:	*CITY OF BANGOR*	BREADTH:	19.9
LOCATION:	Isles of Shoals, New Hampshire	DRAUGHT:	5.0
		GROSS TONNAGE:	159.3
BUILT:	1879 - Barbour Brothers, Brewer, Maine.		
STATUS:	Burned Salem Harbor, Massachusetts, 1894.		

VIKING (2)

ROUTE:	Portsmouth, New Hampshire - Isles of Shoals	NUMBER:	16173
PORTS:	Portsmouth, Isles of Shoals	LENGTH:	114
COMPANY:	Laighton Brothers	BREADTH:	24
		DRAUGHT:	10
		GROSS TONNAGE:	234

BUILT: 1894 - Wilmington, Delaware, Jackson Sharp & Co.

HISTORY: Portsmouth, New Hampshire 1895-1897.
Wilmington, Delaware 1989-1900.

STATUS: Sold to New York and Bermuda Company. In Venezuela used as a yacht. Probably employed as gunboat in the asphalt war. Made run to Port of Spain in nine days. Sold to British June 30, 192

BALTIMORE

ROUTE:	Portsmouth, New Hampshire - Isles of Shoals	NUMBER:	3194
PORTS:	Boston, Isles of Shoals, Portsmouth	LENGTH:	100.0
COMPANY:	Boston & Portsmouth Steamship Co.	BREADTH:	22.0
OTHER NAME:	*POMHAM*	DRAUGHT:	6.8
LOCATION:	Off Portsmouth, New Hampshire	GROSS TONNAGE:	161.0
BUILT:	1881 - Athens, New York.		
HISTORY:	1881-1885 Philadelphia, Pennsylvania.		
	1885-1890 Providence, Rhode Island.		
	1891-1896 Portsmouth, New Hampshire.		
	1917-1930 Providence, Rhode Island.		
STATUS:	Abandoned June 30, 1931.		

SIGHTSEER

ROUTE:	Portsmouth - Isles of Shoals	NUMBER:	127030
PORTS:	Portsmouth, Isles of Shoals	LENGTH:	86.4
COMPANY:	Star Island Steamboat Co.	BREADTH:	21.6
OTHER NAMES:	*CITY OF QUINCY, TANIWHA, TANIWHA* (British)	DRAUGHT:	7.7
LOCATION:	Portsmouth, New Hampshire	GROSS TONNAGE:	97.0
BUILT:	1894 - Braintree, Massachusetts.		

HISTORY: Boston, Massachusetts 1894-1900.
Bermuda 1901-1907.
New York, New York 1907.
New London, Connecticut 1910.
Portsmouth, New Hampshire - Isles of Shoals 1911-1945.

STATUS: Abandoned 1955.

A 21884 Steamboat Merrimac at her Dock, Haverhill, Mass.

MERRIMAC

ROUTE:	Haverhill - Newburyport	NUMBER:	92433
PORTS:	Haverhill, Newburyport	LENGTH:	146.0
COMPANY:	Merrimac Valley Steamboat Co.	BREADTH:	32.0
LOCATION:	Haverhill, Massachusetts	DRAUGHT:	5.7
		GROSS TONNAGE:	211.0

BUILT: 1892 - Lemuel Marquand, Salisbury, Massachusetts.
STATUS: Broken up 1915.

CITY OF HAVERHILL

ROUTE:	Boston - Haverhill	NUMBER:	127661
PORTS:	Haverhill, Newburyport, Gloucester, Boston	LENGTH:	121.7
COMPANY:	Haverhill, Newburyport & Boston	BREADTH:	24.0
	Steamboat Co.	DRAUGHT:	10.7
OTHER NAME:	*MILDRED*	GROSS TONNAGE:	343.0
LOCATION:	Newburyport Harbor		
BUILT:	1902 - East Boston, Massachusetts.		
HISTORY:	Ran 1902-1903. Sold to Key West, Florida group, October 29, 1909.		
STATUS:	Not listed after 1914.		

CITY OF GLOUCESTER

ROUTE: Boston - Gloucester Line
PORTS: Boston, Salem, Gloucester
COMPANY: Boston & Gloucester Steamboat Co.
OTHER NAME: *THAMES*

BUILT: 1884 - Brooklyn, New York.
HISTORY: Sold to Thames River Line, December 2, 1927.

NUMBER: 126139
LENGTH: 142.5
BREADTH: 28.0
DRAUGHT: 11.6
GROSS TONNAGE: 561.0

CAPE ANN

ROUTE:	Boston - Gloucester Line	NUMBER:	127074
PORTS:	Boston, Gloucester	LENGTH:	171.0
COMPANY:	Boston & Gloucester Steamboat Co.	BREADTH:	28.0
OTHER NAME:	(Fr.) *SEMINOLE*	DRAUGHT:	14.2
LOCATION:	Boston Harbor	GROSS TONNAGE:	718.0
BUILT:	1895 - Neafie & Levy & Co., Philadelphia, Pennsylvania.		
STATUS:	Sold to French Government 1920.		

MASCOTTE

ROUTE:	Boston - Gloucester	NUMBER:	91818
PORTS:	Boston, Gloucester	LENGTH:	195.5
COMPANY:	Boston & Gloucester Steamboat Line	BREADTH:	30.0
		DRAUGHT:	19.6
		GROSS TONNAGE:	884.0

BUILT:	1885 - Wm. Cramp & Sons, Philadelphia, Pennsylvania.
HISTORY:	Bought 1923, used until 1925.
STATUS:	Abandoned 1930.

NELLY BAKER

ROUTE: Boston - Nahant
PORTS: Boston, Nahant
COMPANY: Boston & Nahant Steamboat Co.

NUMBER: *
LENGTH: 153.0
BREADTH: 26.0
DRAUGHT: 8.5
GROSS TONNAGE: 303.0

*Official numbering did not begin until 1867.

BUILT: 1854 - Greenpoint, New York.

HISTORY: August 16, 1858, while docked at a Boston wharf, was run into by Philadelphia steamer, *PHINEAS SPRAGUE*, cutting eight feet into the deck. Although the ship was crowded, no passengers were injured.

ADELAIDE

ROUTE:	Boston - Nahant		NUMBER:	25090
PORTS:	Boston, Nahant		LENGTH:	71.0
OTHER NAME:	*UNION*		BREADTH:	18.0
			DRAUGHT:	7.0
			GROSS TONNAGE:	61.27
BUILT:	1864 - Bordentown, New Jersey.			
STATUS:	Abandoned 1917.			

NAHANT

ROUTE: Boston - Nahant
PORTS: Boston, Nahant
COMPANY: Nahant Steamboat Co.
OTHER NAMES: *GENERAL LINCOLN, INDIAN HEAD,*
                 MAYFLOWER
LOCATION: India Wharf, Boston, Massachusetts
BUILT: 1878 - Chelsea, Massachusetts.
HISTORY: 1878-1884 Nahant.
                 1884-1915 Nantasket Beach Steamboat Co.
                 1916-1928 Baltimore, Maryland.
                 1928-1931 Norfolk, Virginia.
STATUS: Abandoned June 30, 1935.

NUMBER: 130126
LENGTH: 160.6
BREADTH: 28.2
DRAUGHT: 8.8
GROSS TONNAGE: 398.60

WINTHROP

ROUTE:	Boston - Winthrop		NUMBER:	81441
PORTS:	Boston, Winthrop		LENGTH:	76.8
COMPANY:	Boston & Winthrop Steamship Co.		BREADTH:	17.6
OTHER NAME:	*MOUNT VERNON*		DRAUGHT:	6.8
			GROSS TONNAGE:	91.0

BUILT: 1893 - Essex, Massachusetts.

HISTORY: Renamed *MOUNT VERNON* May 24, 1929, New York City.

NASSAU

ROUTE:	Boston - Nahant		NUMBER	155325
PORTS:	Boston, Nahant		LENGTH:	133.0
COMPANY:	Boston, Nahant & Pines Steamboat Co.		BREADTH:	26.9
OTHER NAME:	*OLD GLORY*		DRAUGHT:	9.4
			GROSS TONNAGE:	400.0

BUILT: 1898 - Noank, Connecticut.

HISTORY: 1904-1914 Long Island Railroad Co., New York Harbor.
             1914-1916 Boston - Nahant.
             1917 Block Island - Providence.

STATUS: Burned April 26, 1924, at foot of West 155th St., New York City.

Chapter 9

Boston Local Vessels

For a great many years the unique *BOSTON FLOATING HOSPITAL* operated in the outer part of Boston Harbor during the summer. The steamers, *MONITOR, J. PUTNAM BRADLEE, MICHAEL J. PERKINS,* and *STEPHEN O'MEARA* were owned by the City of Boston and served the various institutions in Boston Harbor.

MYRTLE and *KING PHILIP* operated as fishing party steamers out of Boston. *PLEASURE BAY* was a competing steamer from Boston to Nantasket. *CITY OF QUINCY* operated on the Boston to Quincy line for a few years.

The Boston, Revere Beach and Lynn Railroad (narrow gauge) provided a fine ferry service for passengers between East and Downtown Boston. The ferries were: *SWAMPSCOTT, DARTMOUTH, ASHBURNHAM, BREWSTER,* and *NEWTOWN.*

The company changed from coal-burning steam engines to narrow gauge electric cars in later years. The service that had been provided over the years continued with the electric cars being served as usual.

A map of the area is included.

R. Loren Graham

BOSTON FLOATING HOSPITAL

ROUTE:	Boston Harbor	NUMBER:	204283
PORTS:	Maneuvered around Boston Harbor during	LENGTH:	160.3
	Summer months. Tied up at pier during Winter.	BREADTH:	47.0
LOCATION:	Boston Harbor	DRAUGHT:	8.8
		GROSS TONNAGE:	672.0
BUILT:	1906 - Boston, Massachusetts.		
STATUS:	Burned June 1, 1927, in Boston, Massachusetts.		

J. PUTNAM BRADLEE

ROUTE: Boston Harbor Public Institutions
                 on Islands
PORTS: All Boston Harbor Institution Docks
COMPANY: City of Boston, Massachusetts
OTHER NAME: *ADELAIDE*
LOCATION: Boston Harbor
BUILT: 1875 - Lawrence & Foulkes, Greenport, New York.
HISTORY: Sold to William H. Swift, February 23, 1905.

NUMBER: 75820
LENGTH: 140.0
BREADTH: 26.0
DRAUGHT: 8.6
GROSS TONNAGE: 355.7
SPEED: 18 Knots

MONITOR

ROUTE:	Boston Harbor & Islands		NUMBER:	208895
PORTS:	City Owned Piers		LENGTH:	147.6
COMPANY:	City of Boston, Massachusetts		BREADTH:	26.0
OTHER NAME:	*EASTERN SHORE*		DRAUGHT:	9.0
LOCATION:	Boston Harbor		GROSS TONNAGE:	413.0
BUILT:	1904 - Boston, Massachusetts.			
HISTORY:	Renamed *EASTERN SHORE*, August 13, 1923, at Mobile, Alabama.			

MICHAEL J. PERKINS

ROUTE: Boston Harbor & Islands
PORTS: City Owned Piers
COMPANY: City of Boston Public Works Department
OTHER NAME: *GENERAL ROCHESTER*

NUMBER: 222700
LENGTH: 123.1
BREADTH: 28.3
DRAUGHT: 10.7
GROSS TONNAGE: 357.0

BUILT: 1919 - Milwaukee, Wisconsin.
HISTORY: Built for United States Army Transportation Department. Sold to City of Boston in late 1920's.
STATUS: Abandoned 1952.

STEPHEN O'MEARA

ROUTE:	Boston Harbor & Islands	NUMBER:	230496
PORTS:	City Piers	LENGTH:	112.8
COMPANY:	City of Boston, Massachusetts	BREADTH:	22.9
LOCATION:	Boston Harbor	DRAUGHT:	10.8
		GROSS TONNAGE:	183.0
BUILT:	1931 - Boston, Massachusetts.		

MYRTLE

ROUTE:	Boston Harbor for Ocean Fishing Trips	NUMBER:	222752
PORTS:	Boston Harbor & Approaches	LENGTH:	133.7
OTHER NAME:	*U.S.L.H. Steamer MYRTLE*	BREADTH:	25.0
LOCATION:	Boston Harbor	DRAUGHT:	11.0
		GROSS TONNAGE:	236.0

BUILT: 1872 - Philadelphia, Pennsylvania.
STATUS: Abandoned 1944.

F. E. Claes

KING PHILIP

ROUTE:	Boston Harbor Fishing Parties	NUMBER:	161039
PORTS:	Boston Harbor & Approaches	LENGTH:	138.3
COMPANY:	Dixon Steamship Co.	BREADTH:	23.3
LOCATION:	Boston Harbor	DRAUGHT:	8.0
		GROSS TONNAGE:	279.0
BUILT:	1893 - Bath, Maine.		
STATUS:	Abandoned June 30, 1935.		

PLEASURE BAY

ROUTE: Boston - Nantasket
PORTS: Boston, Nantasket
COMPANY: Boston Harbor Steamboat Co.
LOCATION: Boston Harbor

NUMBER: 150495
LENGTH: 150.8
BREADTH: 25.5
DRAUGHT: 7.0
GROSS TONNAGE: 412.97

BUILT: 1890 - Upper Nyack, New York.
HISTORY: 1890-1904 New York Harbor.
             1904 Boston to Quincy and Nantasket, Massachusetts.
             1906 Mobile, Alabama.
STATUS: Burned Madisonville, Louisiana, June 4, 1922.

CITY OF QUINCY

ROUTE:	Boston - Nantasket		NUMBER:	127030
PORTS:	Boston, Quincy, Nantasket		LENGTH:	86.4
COMPANY:	Quincy & Nantasket Steamboat Co.		BREADTH:	23.3
OTHER NAMES:	*TANIWHA, SIGHTSEER*		DRAUGHT:	7.7
LOCATION:	Boston Harbor		GROSS TONNAGE:	111.0
BUILT:	1894 - Braintree, Massachusetts.			
HISTORY:	Portsmouth, New Hampshire to Isles of Shoals 1911-1945.			
STATUS:	Abandoned 1955.			

SWAMPSCOTT

ROUTE:	Boston - East Boston Ferry	NUMBER:	115864
PORTS:	Boston Downtown, East Boston	LENGTH:	124.5
COMPANY:	Boston, Revere Beach & Lynn Railroad Co.	BREADTH:	25.3
LOCATION:	Boston Harbor	DRAUGHT:	10.8
		GROSS TONNAGE:	416.0

BUILT: 1882 - Boston, Massachusetts.

HISTORY: Operated from Portland to Peaks Island in Portland Harbor several years.

Mariners Museum, Newport News, Virginia

DARTMOUTH

ROUTE:	Boston Harbor Ferry	NUMBER:	157548
PORTS:	Downtown Boston, East Boston	LENGTH:	126.6
COMPANY:	Boston, Revere Beach & Lynn Railroad Co.	BREADTH:	27.0
LOCATION:	Crossing Boston Harbor	DRAUGHT:	11.3
		GROSS TONNAGE:	420.0

BUILT: 1899 - William McKie Co., Boston, Massachusetts.
HISTORY: Ran entire life in this service.
STATUS: Sold for scrap June 26, 1940.

Mariners Museum, Newport News, Virginia

ASHBURNHAM

ROUTE:	Boston Harbor Ferry	NUMBER:	201930
PORTS:	Downtown Boston, East Boston	LENGTH:	130.2
COMPANY:	Boston, Revere Beach & Lynn Railroad Co.	BREADTH:	27.5
SISTER SHIPS:	*BREWSTER, NEWTOWN*	DRAUGHT:	11.2
LOCATION:	Crossing from Boston	GROSS TONNAGE:	446.0
	to East Boston, Massachusetts		
BUILT:	1905 - Boston, Massachusetts.		
HISTORY:	Boston, Massachusetts, Ferry entire life.		
STATUS:	Abandoned 1943.		

BREWSTER

ROUTE:	Boston Harbor Ferry	NUMBER:	202999
PORTS:	Downtown Boston, East Boston	LENGTH:	130.5
COMPANY:	Boston, Revere Beach & Lynn Railroad Co.	BREADTH:	27.5
SISTER SHIPS:	*ASHBURNHAM, NEWTOWN*	DRAUGHT:	11.2
LOCATION:	Leaving East Boston for Boston	GROSS TONNAGE:	447.0
BUILT:	1906 - William McKie Co., Boston, Massachusetts.		
HISTORY:	Entire life in Boston Harbor.		
STATUS:	Sold for scrap June 26, 1940.		

NEWTOWN

ROUTE:	Ferry Boston - East Boston	NUMBER:	205073
PORTS:	Downtown Boston, East Boston	LENGTH:	130.5
COMPANY:	Boston, Revere & Lynn Railroad Co.	BREADTH:	27.7
SISTERS SHIPS:	*ASHBURNHAM, BREWSTER*	DRAUGHT:	11.2
LOCATION:	Sailing from East Boston to Boston	GROSS TONNAGE:	447.0
BUILT:	1908 - East Boston, Massachusetts.		
HISTORY:	Entire life in Boston Harbor.		

NANTASKET

Chapter 10

Nantasket and Plymouth Fleet

Early steamers servicing Nantasket were *ROSE STANDISH, GOVERNOR ANDREW, JOHN ROMER, GENERAL LINCOLN, NANTASKET* and *HINGHAM.* For many years the Nantasket Beach Steamboat Company operated the following vessels: *MAYFLOWER, MYLES STANDISH, NANTASKET* (2), *OLD COLONY* (small), SOUTH SHORE, BETTY ALDEN, ROSE STANDISH (2), *MARY CHILTON, NANTASKET* (3), *ALLERTON, PEMBERTON,* and *PLYMOUTH.* They ran between Boston and Plymouth, also from Boston to Hull, Pemberton and Nantasket.

Thanksgiving Day 1929, the steamers: *NANTASKET* (2), *OLD COLONY, BETTY ALDEN, ROSE STANDISH* and *MARY CHILTON* burned at Nantasket. The *MAYFLOWER,* not at the same dock, kept the service going until four ships, *NANTASKET* (3), *ALLERTON, PEMBERTON* and *PLYMOUTH* were purchased to replace those lost.

The company eventually went out of business. Over the years several ships provided service. Among them were the *TOWN OF HULL, FRANCIS SCOTT KEY* and *MOHAWK.*

ROSE STANDISH

ROUTE: Hingham Line
PORTS: Boston, Hingham
COMPANY: Boston & Hingham Steamboat Co.
LOCATION: Boston Harbor

NUMBER: 21130
LENGTH: 151.1
BREADTH: 27.4
DRAUGHT: 8.1
GROSS TONNAGE: 392.0

BUILT: 1863 - Brooklyn, New York.
HISTORY: Sold to Frontier Steamboat Co., Calais, Maine, 1887.
    During Civil War chartered by United States Government. Used to exchange prisoners.
STATUS: Totally destroyed by fire April 20, 1900.

JOHN ROMER

ROUTE:	Boston - Hingham - Nantasket	NUMBER:	12826
PORTS:	Boston, Hingham, Nantasket	LENGTH:	178.0
COMPANY:	Boston & Hingham Steamboat Co.	BREADTH:	26.0
OTHER NAME:	*LOUISE*	DRAUGHT:	8.0
LOCATION:	Boston Wharf	GROSS TONNAGE:	409.0
BUILT:	1863 - Keyport, New Jersey.		

HISTORY: Owned by the Boston & Hingham Steamboat Co., May 13, 1869. Sold, 1883, to Chesapeake & Ohio Railroad Co., Norfolk, as transfer boat between Norfolk and Newport News, Virginia. Collided with a Mud Scow below Norfolk, January 8, 1885. Sunk in fifteen feet of water, dense fog prevailed at the time. No lives lost.

GOVERNOR ANDREW

ROUTE:	Nantasket Line	NUMBER:	85328
PORTS:	Boston, Pemberton, Nantasket	LENGTH:	164.0
COMPANY:	Nantasket Beach Steamboat Co.	BREADTH:	29.0
LOCATION:	Boston Harbor	DRAUGHT:	9.0
		GROSS TONNAGE:	503.0

BUILT: 1874 - Greenport, New York.
STATUS: Burned at Grove's Wharf, East Boston, Massachusetts, June 18, 1911. Two lives lost.

GENERAL LINCOLN

ROUTE: Nantasket Line
PORTS: Boston, Pemberton, Nantasket
COMPANY: Nantasket Beach Steamboat Co.
OTHER NAMES: *NAHANT, INDIAN HEAD, MAYFLOWER*
LOCATION: Boston Harbor
BUILT: 1878 - Chelsea, Massachusetts.
HISTORY: 1878-1884 Nahant, Massachusetts.
1884-1915 Nantasket, Massachusetts.
1916-1928 Baltimore, Maryland.
1928-1930 Norfolk, Virginia.
STATUS: Abandoned June 30, 1935.

NUMBER: 130126
LENGTH: 160.6
BREADTH: 28.2
DRAUGHT: 8.8
GROSS TONNAGE: 398.60

NANTASKET

ROUTE:	Nantasket Line	NUMBER:	130127
PORTS:	Boston, Pemberton, Nantasket	LENGTH:	173.5
COMPANY:	Nantasket Beach Steamboat Co.	BREADTH:	29.1
OTHER NAME:	*KEANSBURG*	DRAUGHT:	9.0
LOCATION:	Boston Harbor	GROSS TONNAGE:	498.22
BUILT:	1878 - Chelsea, Massachusetts.		
HISTORY:	Sold to New York interests, September 17, 1900.		
STATUS:	Burned at Newburgh, New York, April 16, 1928.		

HINGHAM

ROUTE:	Nantasket Line	NUMBER:	96338
PORTS:	Boston, Pemberton, Nantasket	LENGTH:	142.6
COMPANY:	Nantasket Beach Steamboat Co.	BREADTH:	25.0
OTHER NAMES:	*ORIENT, BAY QUEEN*	DRAUGHT:	9.2
		GROSS TONNAGE:	378.58

BUILT: 1896 - Chelsea, Massachusetts.

HISTORY: 1901 sold to Long Island Railroad Co.
                 1923 named *BAY QUEEN* at Mobile, Alabama.

STATUS: Burned at Mobile, March 28, 1929.

MAYFLOWER

ROUTE:	Nantasket Line - Dance Trips	NUMBER:	92291
PORTS:	Boston, Pemberton, Nantasket	LENGTH:	210.0
COMPANY:	Nantasket Beach Steamboat Co.	BREADTH:	32.6
LOCATION:	Boston Harbor	DRAUGHT:	10.4
		GROSS TONNAGE:	786.0

BUILT: 1891 - Montgomery & Howard, Chelsea, Massachusetts.
HISTORY: Steamer in Boston Harbor entire life. Used on Dance Trips occasionally.
STATUS: Restaurant on land near Nantasket, Massachusetts, 1945.

MYLES STANDISH

ROUTE:	Nantasket Line	NUMBER:	92656
PORTS:	Boston, Pemberton, Nantasket	LENGTH:	197.8
COMPANY:	The Nantasket Beach Steamboat Co.	BREADTH:	33.6
LOCATION:	Boston Harbor	DRAUGHT:	10.9
		GROSS TONNAGE:	700.0

BUILT: 1895 - Montgomery & Howard, Chelsea, Massachusetts.

HISTORY: Sold to New York operators, 1924.
                New York - Atlantic Highlands, New Jersey, 1926.

STATUS: Broken up at Kearney, New Jersey, March, 1935.

NANTASKET (2)

ROUTE:	Nantasket Line	NUMBER:	130966
PORTS:	Boston, Pemberton, Nantasket	LENGTH:	203.0
COMPANY:	Nantasket Beach Steamboat Co.	BREADTH:	34.0
LOCATION:	Boston Harbor	GROSS TONNAGE:	739.0

BUILT: 1902 - Montgomery & Howard, Chelsea, Massachusetts.

HISTORY: Entire life in Boston Harbor.

STATUS: Burned at Nantasket, Thanksgiving Day, November 28, 1929, with *OLD COLONY* (small), *MARY CHILTON, BETTY ALDEN, ROSE STANDISH* (2).

OLD COLONY (small)

ROUTE:	Nantasket Line	NUMBER:	200888
PORTS:	Boston, Pemberton, Hull, Nantasket	LENGTH:	190.0
COMPANY:	Nantasket Beach Steamboat Co.	BREADTH:	32.6
LOCATION:	Boston Harbor	DRAUGHT:	11.3
		GROSS TONNAGE:	741.0

BUILT: 1904 - J. K. Montgomery, Chelsea, Massachusetts.

HISTORY: Entire life in Boston Harbor.

STATUS: Burned at Nantasket, Thanksgiving Day, 1929, with *NANTASKET* (2), *MARY CHILTON, BETTY ALDEN, ROSE STANDISH* (2).

Ernest H. Dickson

SOUTH SHORE

ROUTE:	Nantasket Line, also Plymouth Line	NUMBER:	203001
PORTS:	Boston, Pemberton, Nantasket,	LENGTH:	207.0
	also Boston, Plymouth	BREADTH:	32.6
COMPANY:	Nantasket Beach Steamboat Co.	DRAUGHT:	11.6
LOCATION:	Boston Harbor	GROSS TONNAGE:	874.0
BUILT:	1906 - Fore River Shipbuilding Co., Quincy, Massachusetts.		
HISTORY:	Sold to New York operators, 1924.		
STATUS:	Ran ashore south of Atlantic City, New Jersey, April 28, 1928. Later broke up.		

BETTY ALDEN

ROUTE: Nantasket Line, also Plymouth Line
PORTS: Boston, Pemberton, Hull and Nantasket
-also Boston, Plymouth.

COMPANY: Nantasket Beach Steamboat Co.
LOCATION: Boston Harbor with the Gloucester
Steamer, CAPE ANN, in Background.

BUILT: 1908 - Atlantic Works, East Boston, Massachusetts.
HISTORY: Entire life Boston Harbor and Plymouth run.
STATUS: Burned at Nantasket, Thanksgiving Day, 1929, with NANTASKET (2), MARY CHILTON, OLD COLONY (small), ROSE STANDISH (2).

NUMBER:	205108
LENGTH:	190.0
BREADTH:	31.0
DRAUGHT:	11.5
GROSS TONNAGE:	775.0

ROSE STANDISH (2)

ROUTE:	Nantasket Line	NUMBER:	209822
PORTS:	Boston, Pemberton, Nantasket	LENGTH:	215.0
COMPANY:	Nantasket Beach Steamboat Co.	BREADTH:	34.0
LOCATION:	Sailing out of Boston Harbor.	DRAUGHT:	11.4
		GROSS TONNAGE:	993.0

BUILT: 1912 - W. & A. Fletcher Co., Wilmington, Delaware.
HISTORY: Entire life in Boston Harbor.
STATUS: Burned at Nantasket, Thanksgiving Day, 1929, with *OLD COLONY* (small), *BETTY ALDEN*, *NANTASKET* (2), *MARY CHILTON*.

Ernest H. Dickson

MARY CHILTON

ROUTE:	Nantasket Line	NUMBER:	214363
PORTS:	Boston, Pemberton, Nantasket	LENGTH:	205.2
COMPANY:	Nantasket Beach Steamboat Co.	BREADTH:	32.5
LOCATION:	Sailing out of Boston Harbor	DRAUGHT:	12.2
		GROSS TONNAGE:	922.0

BUILT: 1916 - William McKie, East Boston, Massachusetts.

HISTORY: Entire life in Boston Harbor.

STATUS: Burned at Nantasket, Thanksgiving Day, 1929, with *OLD COLONY* (small), *NANTASKET* (2), *BETTY ALDEN*, *ROSE STANDISH* (2).

R. Loren Graham

NANTASKET (3)

ROUTE:	Nantasket Line	NUMBER:	130350
PORTS:	Boston, Nantasket	LENGTH:	200.0
COMPANY:	Nantasket & Boston Steamboat Co.	BREADTH:	32.0
OTHER NAME:	*NEWBURGH*	DRAUGHT:	11.0
LOCATION:	Boston Harbor	GROSS TONNAGE:	1033.0
BUILT:	1887 - Neafie & Levy, Philadelphia, Pennsylvania.		
HISTORY:	Purchased from George T. Ellis, 1930.		
STATUS:	Scrapped at Bordentown, New Jersey, 1955.		

ALLERTON

ROUTE:	Nantasket Line	NUMBER:	95920
PORTS:	Boston, Nantasket	LENGTH:	225.0
COMPANY:	Nantasket & Boston Steamboat Co.	BREADTH:	32.5
OTHER NAME:	*HOMER RAMSDELL*	DRAUGHT:	11.8
LOCATION:	Boston Harbor	GROSS TONNAGE:	1181.0
BUILT:	1887 - T. S. Marvel S. B. Co., Newburgh, New York.		
HISTORY:	Purchased 1930.		
STATUS:	Scrapped at Bordentown, New Jersey, 1952.		

PEMBERTON

ROUTE:	Nantasket Line		NUMBER:	25351
PORTS:	Boston, Nantasket		LENGTH:	178.0
COMPANY:	Nantasket & Boston Steamboat Co.		BREADTH:	31.0
OTHER NAME:	*UNCATENA*		DRAUGHT:	12.0
LOCATION:	Boston Harbor		GROSS TONNAGE:	831.0
BUILT:	1902 - Pusey & Jones Co., Wilmington, Delaware.			
HISTORY:	Purchased, 1930, from Nantucket Line.			
STATUS:	Scrapped at Quincy, Massachusetts, 1937.			

Ernest H. Dickson

PLYMOUTH (2)

OUTE:	Plymouth Line	NUMBER:	93331
ORTS:	Boston, Plymouth.	LENGTH:	200.0
	Special trips to Cape Cod Canal.	BREADTH:	36.0
OMPANY:	Nantasket & Boston Steamboat Co.	DRAUGHT:	11.5
THER NAMES:	*MIDDLESEX, MANHATTAN*	GROSS TONNAGE:	2280.0
OCATION:	Boston Harbor		
UILT:	1902 - Neafie & Levy, Philadelphia, Pennsylvania.		
ISTORY:	*MIDDLESEX* from 1902 to 1929, Ween Steamboat Co., Baltimore, Maryland. *PLYMOUTH*, 1929 to 1937. Renamed *MANHATTAN*, April 26, 1937. Sold as a barge, 1946.		

TOWN OF HULL

ROUTE:	Nantasket Line	NUMBER:	1167
PORTS:	Boston, Nantasket	LENGTH:	226
OTHER NAMES:	*EMPIRE STATE, SHINNECOCK*	BREADTH:	35
LOCATION:	Boston Harbor	DRAUGHT:	14
		GROSS TONNAGE:	1402

BUILT: 1896 - Harlan & Hollingsworth Co., Wilmington, Delaware.
STATUS: Scrapped at Pemberton, Massachusetts, 1946.

FRANCIS SCOTT KEY

ROUTE: Nantasket Line
PORTS: Boston, Nantasket
OTHER NAME: *SUSQUEHANNA*

NUMBER: 116827
LENGTH: 157.7
BREADTH: 38.0
DRAUGHT: 9.0
GROSS TONNAGE: 462.0

BUILT: 1898 - C. Reeders & Sons, Baltimore, Maryland.
HISTORY: 1898-1923 Baltimore, Maryland.
1923-1941 New Orleans, Louisiana.
1941-1943 Baltimore, Maryland.
1944-1946 New York, New York.
1947 Baltimore, Maryland.
1948 Boston, Massachusetts.
STATUS: Scrapped at Bordentown, New Jersey, 1952.

MOHAWK

ROUTE:	Nantasket Line	NUMBER:	201088
PORTS:	Boston, Nantasket	LENGTH:	174.0
OTHER NAME:	*ANNE ARUNDEL*	BREADTH:	36.0
		DRAUGHT:	10.2
		GROSS TONNAGE:	419.0

BUILT: 1904 - Baltimore S. B. & D. D. Co., Baltimore, Maryland.

HISTORY: *ANNE ARUNDEL* from 1904 to 1937, Weens Steamboat Co. *MOHAWK*, 1938 to 1948 in Boston. 1948-1952, laid up.

STATUS: Scrapped at Baltimore, 1952.

Chapter 11

South of Boston Vessels

From 1897 to 1899 a competing service was established from Boston to Plymouth, with the steamer *PLYMOUTH*. The following vessels ran from Boston to Provincetown: *LONGFELLOW, CAPE COD, DOROTHY BRADFORD, STEEL PIER, GOVERNOR COBB, NORUMBEGA, ROMANCE, HOLIDAY.* This was a very popular vacation trip during the summer.

Passenger vessels leaving Boston en route to Plymouth, Cape Cod Canal, or Provincetown, passed Minot's Ledge Lighthouse, located on the south shore of Greater Boston. The granite shaft lighthouse has the call numbers 1 - 4 - 3.

Early in its history a young lighthouse keeper had a sweetheart living on the shore who could look out at Minot's Light, which at that time was a steady light. Each night the young man would signal to his sweetheart by placing a blanket over one side of the light giving the signal 1 - 4 - 3, which means "I love you."

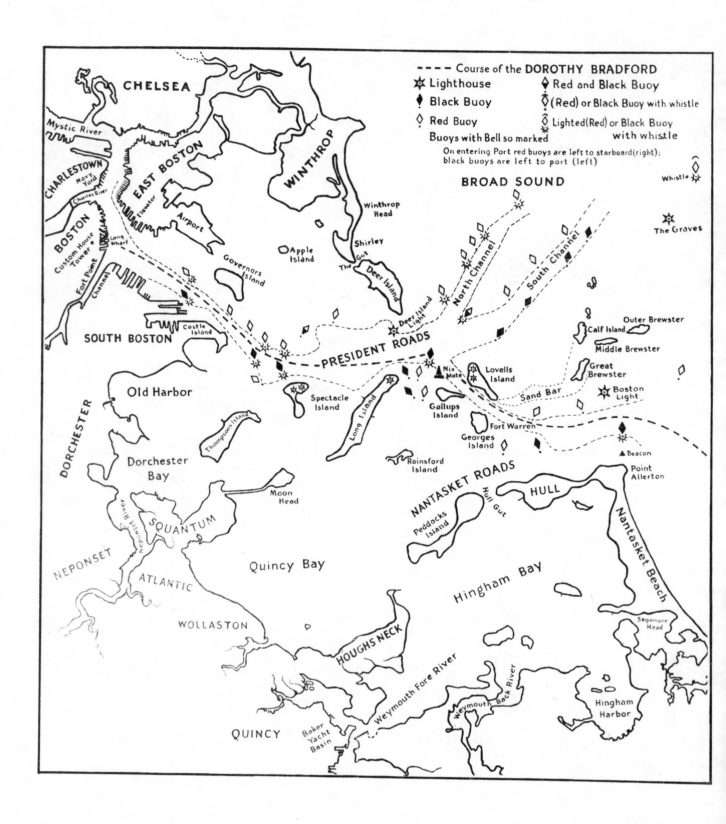

CHELSEA

Mystic River

CHARLESTOWN
Navy Yard
Charles River

EAST BOSTON

WINTHROP

Winthrop
Head

BROAD SOUND

- - - - Course of the DOROTHY BRADFORD
✦ Lighthouse ◆ Red and Black Buoy
◆ Black Buoy ◈ (Red) or Black Buoy with whistle
◇ Red Buoy ◈ Lighted(Red) or Black Buoy
Buoys with Bell so marked with whistle

On entering Port red buoys are left to starboard(right);
black buoys are left to port (left)

Whistle

The Graves

BOSTON
Custom House
Tower
Fort Point
Long Wharf
Elevator
Airport

Governors
Island

Apple
Island

Shirley

The Gut

Deer Island

Deer Island
Light

North Channel

South Channel

Outer Brewster

Calf Island

Middle Brewster

SOUTH BOSTON

Castle
Island

PRESIDENT ROADS

Nix
Mate

Lovells
Island

Great
Brewster

Sand Bar

Boston
Light

Old Harbor

Spectacle
Island

Long Island

Gallups
Island

Fort Warren

DORCHESTER

Thompsons Island

Georges
Island

Rainsford
Island

NANTASKET ROADS

Beacon

Point
Allerton

Dorchester
Bay

Moon
Head

HULL

Peddocks
Island

Hull Gut

Sagamore
Head

NEPONSET

Neponset River

SQUANTUM

ATLANTIC

Quincy Bay

Hingham Bay

Nantasket Beach

WOLLASTON

HOUGHS NECK

Weymouth Fore River

Weymouth Back River

Hingham
Harbor

QUINCY

Baker
Yacht
Basin

PLYMOUTH

ROUTE:	Boston - Plymouth	NUMBER:	150754
PORTS:	Boston, Plymouth	LENGTH:	142.0
COMPANY:	Winthrop Steamboat Co.	BREADTH:	30.0
OTHER NAMES:	U.S. Lighthouse Tender - *IRIS*,	DRAUGHT:	10.4
	Motor Vessel - *BIG CHIEF*	GROSS TONNAGE:	428.0
LOCATION:	At a Dock in Plymouth Harbor, Massachusetts		
BUILT:	1897 - Neafie & Levy, Philadelphia, Pennsylvania.		

HISTORY: Ran Boston to Plymouth, Massachusetts, 1897-1899. Sold to United States Government for U.S. Lighthouse Tender named *IRIS*. Purchased by unknown party from United States Government, February, 1939.

LONGFELLOW

ROUTE:	The Provincetown Line	NUMBER:	140626
PORTS:	Boston, Provincetown	LENGTH:	146.5
LOCATION:	Provincetown Harbor, Massachusetts	BREADTH:	27.0
		DRAUGHT:	12.4
		GROSS TONNAGE:	413.1

BUILT: 1883 - Boston, Massachusetts.

HISTORY: 1885, Mount Desert Ferry and Annapolis, Nova Scotia. May 12, 1903, owned by New York and
Puerto Rican Steamship Co. October 5, 1904, crossing Nantucket Shoals, sprang a leak and
foundered off Pamet River Life Saving Station.

CAPE COD

ROUTE:	Provincetown Line	NUMBER:	127452
PORTS:	Boston, Provincetown	LENGTH:	151.0
	Also Boston, Plymouth	BREADTH:	32.1
COMPANY:	Boston, Plymouth & Provincetown Co.	DRAUGHT:	12.5
		GROSS TONNAGE:	557.0
		SPEED:	15 Knots

BUILT: 1900 - Essex, Massachusetts.

HISTORY: Sold to New York parties May 8, 1913. 1926 - Thames River Line.

R. Loren Graham

DOROTHY BRADFORD

ROUTE: Provincetown Line
PORTS: Boston, Provincetown
COMPANY: Cape Cod Steamship Co.
OTHER NAME: *CHARLOTTE*
LOCATION: Boston Harbor, Massachusetts

NUMBER: 126597
LENGTH: 228.9
BREADTH: 38.0
DRAUGHT: 22.0
GROSS TONNAGE: 1746.0

BUILT: 1889 - Neafie & Levy & Co., Philadelphia, Pennsylvania.
HISTORY: *CHARLOTTE*, 1889-1911, Chesapeake Steamship Co.
                DOROTHY BRADFORD, 1911-1935, Boston to Provincetown, and 1935-1937, Philadelphia -
                Bundick's, Virginia, for Atlantic States Line.
STATUS: Ran during 1935. Sold for scrap, June 30, 1937.

STEEL PIER

ROUTE:	Provincetown Line	NUMBER:	92830
PORTS:	Boston, Provincetown	LENGTH:	239.2
COMPANY:	Massachusetts Steamships Lines, Inc.	BREADTH:	40.1
OTHER NAME:	*MIAMI*	DRAUGHT:	21.8
LOCATION:	Boston Harbor	GROSS TONNAGE:	1767.0
		SPEED:	13½ Knots

BUILT: 1897 - Wm. Cramp & Sons, S. B. & E. Co., Philadelphia, Pennsylvania.

HISTORY: 1897-1900, luxury yacht for Henry M. Flagler.
1900-1932, Miami and Nassau, also Key West and Havana.
Bought, 1934, for Provincetown Line. For a while anchored off Atlantic City, New Jersey, which gave her the name *STEEL PIER*.

STATUS: Broken up, 1948, in Baltimore, Maryland.

NORUMBEGA

ROUTE:	Provincetown Line	NUMBER:	130979
PORTS:	Boston, Provincetown	LENGTH:	146.0
COMPANY:	Bay State Steamship Co.	BREADTH:	28.6
OTHER NAME:	*ROMANCE*	DRAUGHT:	10.1
LOCATION:	Passing through Cape Cod Canal	GROSS TONNAGE:	304.0
	in Massachusetts	SPEED:	14.4 Knots
BUILT:	1902 - Bath, Maine.		
HISTORY:	Left Maine Central Railroad, 1928.		
STATUS:	Burned at Quincy, Massachusetts, May, 1944.		

ROMANCE

ROUTE:	Provincetown Line	NUMBER:	145783
PORTS:	Boston, Provincetown	LENGTH:	245.0
COMPANY:	Charles L. Ellis	BREADTH:	38.0
OTHER NAME:	*TENNESSEE*	DRAUGHT:	15.8
		GROSS TONNAGE:	1240.0

BUILT: 1898 - Harlan & Hollingsworth Co., Wilmington, Delaware.

HISTORY: Built for Old Bay Line, Baltimore, Maryland. Sold to Joy Line in New York, 1906.

STATUS: Sunk in Boston Harbor, September 9, 1936, by Eastern Steamship Lines' Steamer *NEW YORK*.
Total loss.

Ernest H. Dickson

HOLIDAY

ROUTE:	Provincetown Line	NUMBER:	228015
PORTS:	Boston, Provincetown	LENGTH:	291.0
OTHER NAMES:	*VIRGINIA LEE, ACCOMAC*	BREADTH:	50.0
		DRAUGHT:	16.5
		GROSS TONNAGE:	21.58

BUILT: 1928 - Bethlehem Steel Shipbuilding Corp., Quincy, Massachusetts.

HISTORY: Built for Cape Charles to Norfolk service. During World War II used in South American service. Boston - Provincetown, 1949-1950.

STATUS: Afloat at Norfolk, Virginia, 1968.

Chapter 12

Plant Line Fleet

A merger of Canadian interests at Halifax, Nova Scotia, formed the Canada, Atlantic and Plant Steamship Company in 1892. The Canada, Atlantic Steamship Company and Mr. H. B. Plant, who owned large railroad interests in Florida, merged and formed the Plant Line. Mr. Plant used his excellent *OLIVETTE*, which earlier had been used on the direct service to Bar Harbor. Later he had the *LA GRANDE DUCHESS*. The Canadian group contributed the *HALIFAX*, the *A. W. PERRY*, and later the new *EVANGELINE*.

This service operated until 1917, when other interests served the Boston-Halifax group.

In 1912 the new *EVANGELINE* came into service under the Canadian flag. She was considered the ultimate in design. In her later years she sailed under the American flag and was last registered in 1918.

A. W. PERRY (Canadian)

ROUTE:	Boston - Halifax	NUMBER:	107635
PORTS:	Boston, Halifax, Nova Scotia	LENGTH:	255.0
COMPANY:	Canada, Atlantic & Plant	BREADTH:	34.0
	Steamship Co., Ltd.	DRAUGHT:	22.0
OTHER NAME:	BEVERLY	GROSS TONNAGE:	1601.0
BUILT:	1897 - Workman, Clark & Co., Ltd., Belfast, Ireland.		
STATUS:	Wrecked June 8, 1915, near Halifax, Nova Scotia.		

W. H. Ballard

OLIVETTE

ROUTE:	Boston - Halifax	NUMBER:	155138
PORTS:	Boston, Halifax, Nova Scotia	LENGTH:	274.3
COMPANY:	Plant Line	BREADTH:	35.2
LOCATION:	Leaving Boston Harbor	DRAUGHT:	11.9
		GROSS TONNAGE:	1611.0
		SPEED:	18 Knots

BUILT:	1877 - Wm. Cramp & Sons, Co., Philadelphia, Pennsylvania.
HISTORY:	Nearly entire life with Plant Line sailing out of Florida.
STATUS:	Total loss on Cuban coast near Havana, January 12, 1918.

HALIFAX (Canadian)

ROUTE:	Boston - Halifax	NUMBER:	95099
PORTS:	Boston, Halifax, Nova Scotia	LENGTH:	250.3
COMPANY:	Canada, Atlantic & Plant Steamship Co. Ltd.	BREADTH:	35.0
		DRAUGHT:	21.5
		GROSS TONNAGE:	1875.0
BUILT:	1888 - London and Glasgow Co. Ltd., Glasgow, Scotland.		
STATUS:	Missing after leaving New York for port in England, 1918.		

EVANGELINE (Canadian)

ROUTE:	Boston - Halifax		NUMBER:	130598
PORTS:	Boston, Halifax, Nova Scotia		LENGTH:	350.7
COMPANY:	Atlantic & Plant Steamship Co. Ltd.		BREADTH:	46.0
			DRAUGHT:	30.3
			GROSS TONNAGE:	4360.0

BUILT: 1912 - London & Glasgow Co., Glasgow, Scotland.
HISTORY: Under American flag, 1914.
STATUS: Wrecked January 14, 1921, Port Louis, France.

LA GRANDE DUCHESSE

ROUTE: Plant Line
PORTS: Boston and Halifax, Nova Scotia
COMPANY: Plant Railroad & Steamship Co.
OTHER NAMES: *CITY OF SAVANNAH, CAROLINA*
LOCATION: Boston Harbor

NUMBER: 141440
LENGTH: 380.0
BREADTH: 47.8
DRAUGHT: 16.5
GROSS TONNAGE: 5018.0
SPEED: 20 Knots

BUILT: 1896 - Newport News Shipbuilding Co.
HISTORY: Ran April to October, 1899. Attended International Yacht races off Sandy Hook, October 3, 1899. Plant Line services from Florida, 1896 to 1901. Sold to Ocean Steamship Co. of Savannah, Georgia, 1901, renamed *CITY OF SAVANNAH*. Sold to New York and Puerto Rico Line, December 28, 1905. Renamed *CAROLINA*.
STATUS: Sunk by German submarine, June 2, 1918, off Cape May, New Jersey.

Chapter 13

The Merchants and Miners Transportation Company

The company was incorporated April 24, 1852, by a group of men from Baltimore and Boston who secured several ships and started the service.

In 1906 the Winsor Line (Boston - Philadelphia) was acquired. Baltimore to Savannah, Jacksonville, and later Miami, as ports of call, were added in 1909.

During the Spanish American War the company operated a fleet of twelve steamers. This was a good company providing excellent service. A fatal accident occurred only once in eighty-seven years.

The last sailing from Boston to Baltimore was on October 18, 1941.

The steamships were: *PERSIAN, PARTHIAN, INDIAN, CHATHAM, ESSEX, GLOUCESTER, HOWARD, JUNIATA, NANTUCKET, GRECIAN, ONTARIO, SOMERSET, ALLEGHANY, BERKSHIRE, CHATHAM* (2), *DORCHESTER, FAIRFAX, IRWIN* and *KENT.*

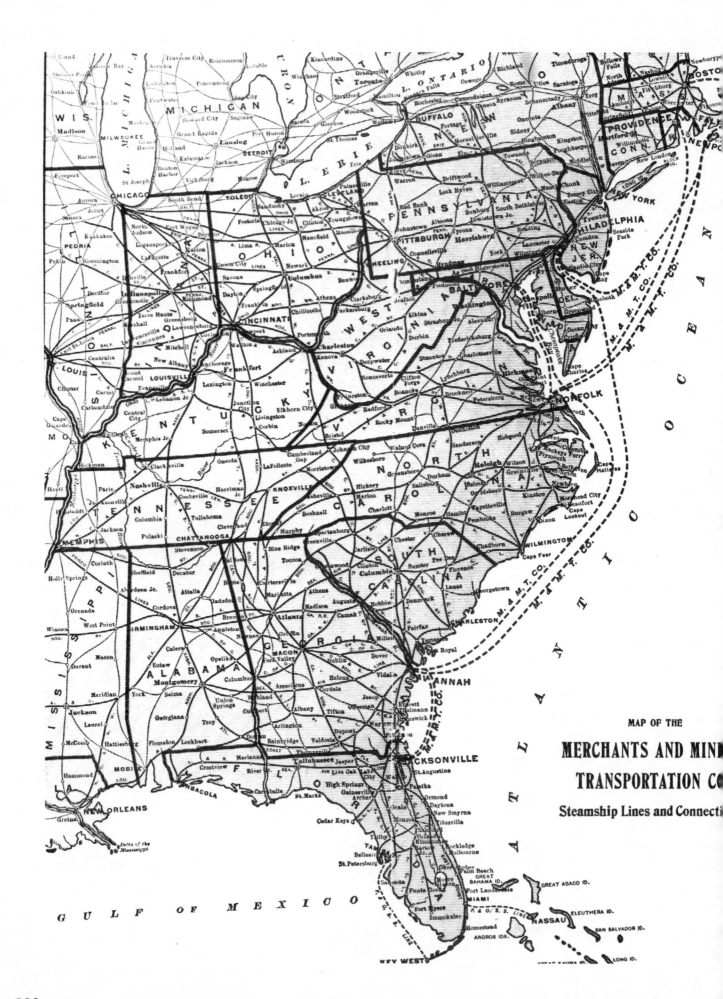

MAP OF THE

MERCHANTS AND MIN[...]

TRANSPORTATION CO[...]

Steamship Lines and Connecti[...]

PERSIAN

ROUTE:	Boston - Philadelphia	NUMBER:	145320
PORTS:	Boston, Philadelphia	LENGTH:	280.0
COMPANY:	Merchants & Miners Transportation Co.	BREADTH:	40.7
OTHER NAME:	*TALLAHASSEE*	DRAUGHT:	15.8
		GROSS TONNAGE:	4180.0

BUILT:	1882 - Chester, Pennsylvania.
HISTORY:	Built for Savannah Line as *TALLAHASSEE*.
STATUS:	Junked, 1928, Boston Iron & Metal Co., Baltimore, Maryland.

PARTHIAN

ROUTE:	Boston - Philadelphia	NUMBER:	1504(
PORTS:	Boston, Philadelphia	LENGTH:	267
COMPANY:	Merchants & Miners Transportation Co.	BREADTH:	38
		DRAUGHT:	16
		GROSS TONNAGE:	1683.1

BUILT: 1887 - Harlan & Hollingsworth Co., Wilmington, Delaware.

HISTORY: Built for Boston & Philadelphia Steamship Co.
Sold to Pennsylvania Sugar Co., July 23, 1917.
Sold to Olympia Shipping Co., January, 1918.

STATUS: Beached after collision on coast of North Africa (Oran), July 25, 1921.

R. Loren Graham

INDIAN

ROUTE:	Boston - Philadelphia	NUMBER:	100465
PORTS:	Boston, Philadelphia	LENGTH:	267.8
COMPANY:	Merchants & Miners Transportation Co.	BREADTH:	38.0
LOCATION:	Boston Harbor	DRAUGHT:	26.0
		GROSS TONNAGE:	1576.0
		SPEED:	14 Knots

BUILT: 1890 - Harlan & Hollingsworth Co., Wilmington, Delaware.

HISTORY: Boston - Philadelphia Line, 1890-1907.
Merchants & Miners Transportation Co., 1907-1928.
Lengthened forty feet at Wilmington, Delaware, 1900.

STATUS: Sold to Boston Iron & Metal Co., Baltimore, Maryland, for scraps, March 28, 1928.

CHATHAM

ROUTE:	Boston - Baltimore	NUMBER:	126269
PORTS:	Boston, Norfolk, Baltimore	LENGTH:	265.4
COMPANY:	Merchants & Miners Transportation Co.	BREADTH:	40.0
OTHER NAMES:	*U.S.S. VULCAN*	DRAUGHT:	15.6
		GROSS TONNAGE:	2728.7
		SPEED:	13 Knots

BUILT: 1884 - American Shipbuilding Co., Philadelphia, Pennsylvania.

HISTORY: Sold to United States Navy Department, May 2, 1898, for fleet repair ship. Renamed *CHATHAM*, August 3, 1899.

STATUS: Wrecked, March 15, 1910, at entrance to St. Johns River, Florida. New owner did not float her. Total loss.

The Society for the Preservation of New England Antiquities

ESSEX

ROUTE:	Boston - Baltimore		NUMBER:	136138
PORTS:	Boston, Norfolk, Baltimore		LENGTH:	318.0
COMPANY:	Merchants & Miners Transportation Co.		BREADTH:	40.0
			DRAUGHT:	23.7
			GROSS TONNAGE:	3018.0
			SPEED:	13 Knots

BUILT: 1890 - Wm. Cramp & Sons, Philadelphia, Pennsylvania.

HISTORY: Lengthened twenty-five feet at Newport News, Virginia, 1906.

STATUS: Lost off Block Island, September 26, 1941.

GLOUCESTER

ROUTE: Boston - Philadelphia
PORTS: Boston, Philadelphia
COMPANY: Merchants & Miners Transportation Co.
LOCATION: Entering Boston Harbor

NUMBER: 86269
LENGTH: 272.7
BREADTH: 42.0
DRAUGHT: 16.0
GROSS TONNAGE: 2541.0
SPEED: 14½ Knots

BUILT: 1893 - Maryland Steel Co., Sparrows Point, Maryland.
HISTORY: United States Transport during Spanish American War.
STATUS: Junked, February, 1938.

HOWARD

ROUTE:	Boston - Philadelphia	NUMBER:	96308
PORTS:	Boston, Philadelphia	LENGTH:	310.5
COMPANY:	Merchants & Miners Transportation Co.	BREADTH:	42.0
LOCATION:	Sailing out of Boston Harbor	DRAUGHT:	26.0
		GROSS TONNAGE:	3581.0

BUILT: 1895 - Harlan & Hollingsworth Co., Wilmington, Delaware.

HISTORY: Lengthened 1909. Last sailing from Boston, October 18, 1941. Owned by United Fruit Subsidiary under Honduran Flag.

STATUS: Scrapped, 1947.

JUNIATA

ROUTE:	Boston - Baltimore	NUMBER:		77274
PORTS:	Boston, Norfolk, Baltimore	LENGTH:		310.0
COMPANY:	Merchants & Miners Transportation Co.	BREADTH:		42.0
		DRAUGHT:		26.0
		GROSS TONNAGE:		3465.0
		SPEED:		17 Knots
BUILT:	1897 - Harlan & Hollingsworth Co., Wilmington, Delaware.			
HISTORY:	Owned by United Fruit Subsidiary under Honduran Registry.			
STATUS:	Scrapped 1947.			

NANTUCKET

ROUTE:	Boston - Norfolk - Newport News - Baltimore	NUMBER:	13815
		LENGTH:	298.0
PORTS:	Boston, Norfolk, Newport News, Baltimore	BREADTH:	42.0
COMPANY:	Merchants & Miners Transportation Co.	DRAUGHT:	16.2
		GROSS TONNAGE:	4315.0

BUILT: 1899 - Harlan & Hollingsworth Co., Wilmington, Delaware.

STATUS: Sunk May 31, 1928, west of East Chop Lighthouse. Hull was blown up.

GRECIAN

ROUTE: Boston - Philadelphia
PORTS: Boston, Philadelphia
COMPANY: Merchants & Miners Transportation Co.

NUMBER: 86491
LENGTH: 290.0
BREADTH: 42.0
DRAUGHT: 36.0
GROSS TONNAGE: 4010.0

BUILT: 1900 - Harlan & Hollingsworth Co., Wilmington, Delaware.
STATUS: Sunk in dense fog off Block Island, May 27, 1932, Four lives lost.

ONTARIO

ROUTE:	Boston - Baltimore	NUMBER:	201169
PORTS:	Boston, Norfolk, Newport News, Baltimore	LENGTH:	315.0
COMPANY:	Merchants & Miners Transportation Co.	BREADTH:	42.0
LOCATION:	Boston Harbor	DRAUGHT:	15.9
		GROSS TONNAGE:	4380.0
		SPEED:	17 Knots

BUILT: 1904 - New York Shipbuilding Co., Camden, New Jersey.

HISTORY: Ran as freighter Boston - Philadelphia, 1941.
1942, sold to a Honduran Subsidiary of the United Fruit Company.

STATUS: Sunk by torpedo near Mobile, Alabama.

SOMERSET

ROUTE:	Boston - Baltimore	NUMBER:	20838
PORTS:	Boston, Norfolk, Newport News, Baltimore	LENGTH:	309.
COMPANY:	Merchants & Miners Transportation Co.	BREADTH:	46.
OTHER NAMES:	*SUWANNEE, CITY OF ROME, VERAMAR*	DRAUGHT:	19.
		GROSS TONNAGE:	3648.0

BUILT: 1911 - New York Shipbuilding Co., Camden, New Jersey, March 30.

HISTORY: Purchased by Savannah Line, 1917. As *CITY OF ROME*, sank United States Submarine S-51.

STATUS: Junked at Baltimore, Maryland, 1938.

R. Loren Graham

ALLEGHANY

ROUTE:	Merchants & Miners Service	NUMBER:	222760
	South of Boston	LENGTH:	368.0
PORTS:	Boston, Norfolk, Newport News,	BREADTH:	52.1
	Baltimore, Philadelphia, Miami	DRAUGHT:	15.2
COMPANY:	Merchants & Miners Transportation Co.	GROSS TONNAGE:	6950.0
OTHER NAME:	*AMERICAN SEAFARER*	SPEED:	13 Knots
SISTER SHIP:	*BERKSHIRE*		
BUILT:	1922 - Federal Shipbuilding Co., Kearny, New Jersey.		
HISTORY:	Delivered to United States Government for War service, November, 1941.		
STATUS:	Scrapped 1949.		

BERKSHIRE

ROUTE:	Merchants & Miners Service	NUMBER:	222831
	South of Boston	LENGTH:	368.0
PORTS:	Boston, Norfolk, Newport News,	BREADTH:	52.0
	Baltimore, Philadelphia, Miami	DRAUGHT:	17.2
COMPANY:	Merchants & Miners Transportation Co.	GROSS TONNAGE:	6950.0
OTHER NAME:	*AMERICAN ENGINEER*	SPEED:	13 Knots
SISTER SHIP:	*ALLEGHANY*		

BUILT: 1923 - Federal Shipbuilding Co., Kearny, New Jersey.

HISTORY: Delivered to United States Government for War service, November, 1941.

STATUS: Scrapped at San Francisco, July, 1948.

Steamship Historical Society of America, Inc.

CHATHAM (2)

ROUTE:	Merchants & Miners Service	NUMBER:	225471
	South of Boston	LENGTH:	368.0
PORTS:	Boston, Norfolk, Newport News,	BREADTH:	52.2
	Baltimore, Philadelphia, Miami	DRAUGHT:	16.0
COMPANY:	Merchants & Miners Transportation Co.	GROSS TONNAGE:	7000.0
SISTER SHIPS:	*DORCHESTER, FAIRFAX*	SPEED:	16 Knots

BUILT: 1925 - Newport News Shipbuilding Co, Newport News, Virginia.

HISTORY: Delivered to United States Government for War service in 1941.

STATUS: Torpedoed in the Strait of Belle Isle, August 27, 1942.

DORCHESTER

ROUTE:	Merchants & Miners Service	NUMBER:	22575
	South of Boston	LENGTH:	368.0
PORTS:	Boston, Norfolk, Newport News,	BREADTH:	52.0
	Baltimore, Philadelphia, Miami	DRAUGHT:	16.0
COMPANY:	Merchants & Miners Transportation Co.	GROSS TONNAGE:	7000.0
SISTER SHIPS:	*CHATHAM, FAIRFAX*	SPEED:	16 Knots

BUILT: 1925 - Newport News Shipbuilding Co., Newport News, Virginia.

HISTORY: Delivered to United States Government for War service, November 1, 1941.

STATUS: Torpedoed February 3, 1943, by U-boat off the coast of Newfoundland. Four Chaplains on this ship became famous by sacrificing their lives so that others might live.

FAIRFAX

ROUTE:	Merchants & Miners Service	NUMBER:	225957
	South of Boston	LENGTH:	368.0
PORTS:	Boston, Norfolk, Newport News,	BREADTH:	52.0
	Baltimore, Philadelphia, Miami	DRAUGHT:	16.0
COMPANY:	Merchants & Miners Transportation Co.	GROSS TONNAGE:	7000.0
OTHER NAMES:	CHUNG HSING, PACIFIC STAR,	SPEED:	16 Knots
	BINTANG SAMUDRA		
SISTER SHIPS:	CHATHAM, DORCHESTER		

BUILT: 1925 - Newport News Shipbuilding Co., Newport News, Virginia.

HISTORY: Delivered to United States Government for War service, October, 1941. Sold to Chinese, 1946. She has flown the American Flag, Chinese Flag, Panamanian Flag, Indonesian Flag.

STATUS: Sold 1951 to Indonesia.

IRWIN

ROUTE:	Boston - Philadelphia	NUMBER:	21588
PORTS:	Boston, Philadelphia	LENGTH:	360
COMPANY:	Merchants & Miners Transportation Co.	BREADTH:	51
OTHER NAMES:	*SANTA CECILIA, SANTA ANA,*	DRAUGHT:	22
	GUATEMALA, JOHN L. CLEM	GROSS TONNAGE:	4900
SISTER SHIP:	*KENT*	SPEED:	12 Kno
BUILT:	1917 - Philadelphia, Pennsylvania, for W. R. Grace Company.		
HISTORY:	Purchased, 1936, from Grace Line.		
	Purchased by United States Government for War service, March 6, 1941.		
STATUS:	Broken up 1948.		

KENT

ROUTE:	Boston - Philadelphia	NUMBER:	216969
PORTS:	Boston, Philadelphia	LENGTH:	360.2
COMPANY:	Merchants & Miners Transportation Co.	BREADTH:	51.6
OTHER NAMES:	*SANTA TERESA, ERNEST HINDS*	DRAUGHT:	22.8
SISTER SHIP:	*IRWIN*	GROSS TONNAGE:	4900.0
		SPEED:	12 Knots

BUILT: 1918 - Philadelphia, Pennsylvania, for W. R. Grace Company.

HISTORY: Purchased, 1936, by Merchants & Miners Transportation Co.
                  Purchased by United States Government for War service, March 6, 1941.

STATUS: Broken up 1959.

Chapter 14

Savannah Line Fleet

The Savannah Line was organized in 1872, as the Ocean Steamship Company of Savannah, Georgia. Colonel William M. Wadley was the first president.

The ships in the fleet shown in this chapter are: *CITY OF SAVANNAH, CITY OF MACON, CITY OF ATLANTA, CITY OF COLUMBUS, CITY OF SAVANNAH* (2), *CITY OF ATHENS, CITY OF ROME, CITY OF MONTGOMERY, CITY OF ST. LOUIS, CITY OF BIRMINGHAM, CITY OF CHATTANOOGA.*

Originally there were two prominent services: Savannah, Georgia, to New York City; and Savannah to Boston, Massachusetts. During the period between World Wars I and II these two services were combined and the steamers sailed from Savannah to New York and then to Boston, returning to New York and back to Savannah.

Because the line was controlled by railroad interests owning coal mines, the steamers were all coal burners.

Service was terminated shortly before World War II.

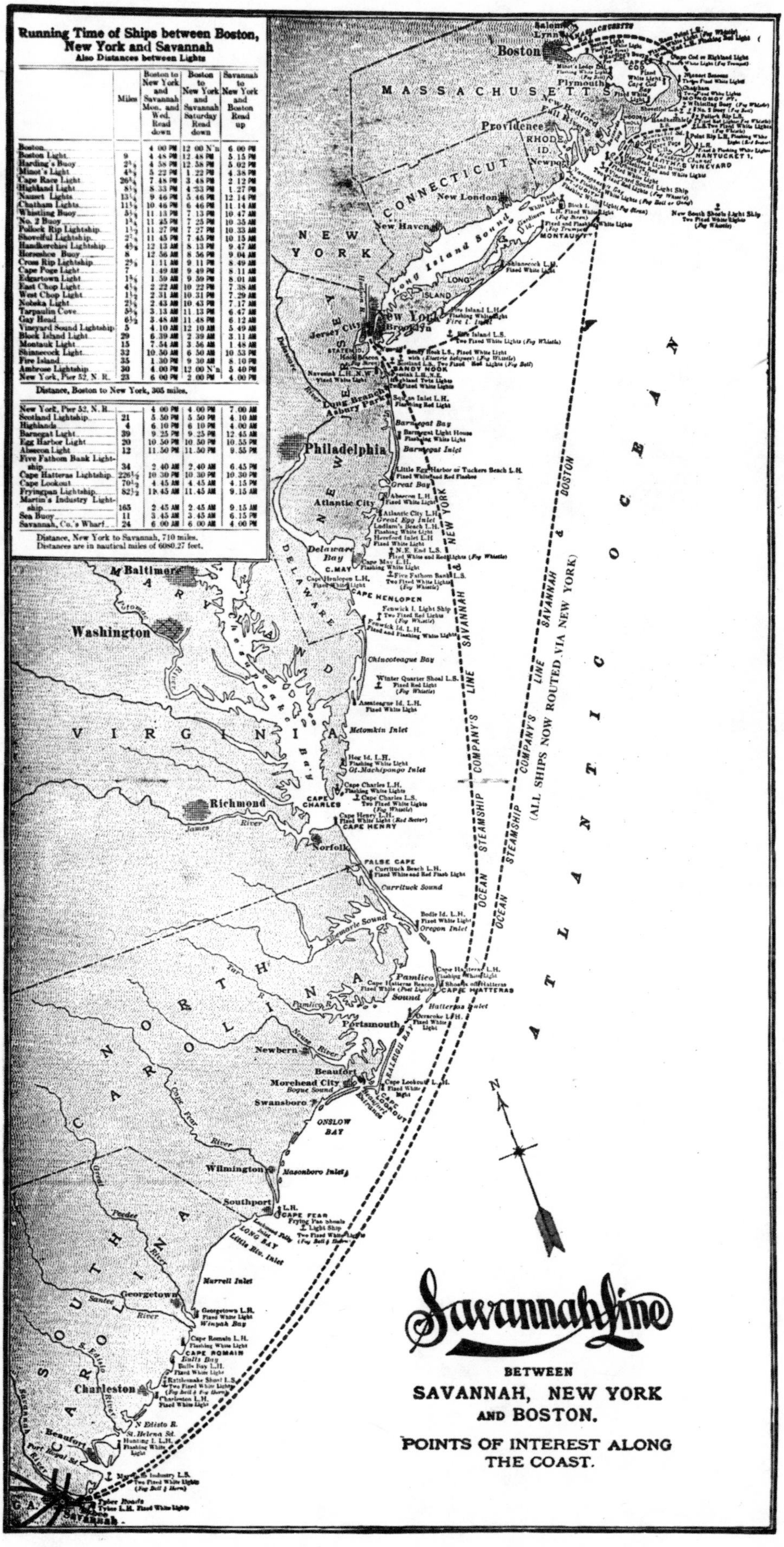

Running Time of Ships between Boston, New York and Savannah

Also Distances between Lights

	Miles	Boston to New York and Savannah Mon. and Wed. Read down	Boston to New York and Savannah Saturday Read down	Savannah to New York and Boston Read up
Boston		4 00 PM	12 00 N'n	6 00 PM
Boston Light	9	4 48 PM	12 48 PM	5 15 PM
Harding's Buoy	2 3/8	4 58 PM	12 58 PM	5 02 PM
Minot's Light	4 3/8	5 22 PM	1 22 PM	4 38 PM
Cape Race Light	26 3/4	7 48 PM	3 48 PM	2 12 PM
Highland Light	8 1/8	8 33 PM	4 33 PM	1 27 PM
Nauset Lights	13 1/4	9 46 PM	5 46 PM	12 14 PM
Chatham Lights	11 1/8	10 46 PM	6 46 PM	11 14 AM
Whistling Buoy	3 1/8	11 13 PM	7 13 PM	10 47 AM
No. 2 Buoy	1 3/4	11 25 PM	7 25 PM	10 35 AM
Pollock Rip Lightship	1 1/2	11 27 PM	7 27 PM	10 33 AM
Shovelful Lightship	2 7/8	11 45 PM	7 45 PM	10 15 AM
Handkerchief Lightship	4 3/8	12 13 AM	8 13 PM	9 47 AM
Horseshoe Buoy	8	12 56 AM	8 56 PM	9 04 AM
Cross Rip Lightship	2 5/8	1 11 AM	9 11 PM	8 49 AM
Cape Poge Light	7	1 49 AM	9 49 PM	8 11 AM
Edgartown Light	1 5/8	1 59 AM	9 59 PM	8 01 AM
East Chop Light	4 1/8	2 22 AM	10 22 PM	7 38 AM
West Chop Light	1 1/2	2 31 AM	10 31 PM	7 29 AM
Nobska Light	2 5/8	2 43 AM	10 43 PM	7 17 AM
Tarpaulin Cove	5 5/8	3 13 AM	11 13 PM	6 47 AM
Gay Head	6 1/2	3 48 AM	11 48 PM	6 12 AM
Vineyard Sound Lightship	5	4 10 AM	12 10 AM	5 49 AM
Block Island Light	29	6 39 AM	2 39 AM	3 11 AM
Montauk Light	15	7 54 AM	3 56 AM	1 48 AM
Shinnecock Light	32	10 50 AM	6 50 AM	10 53 PM
Fire Island	35	1 30 PM	9 30 AM	8 10 PM
Ambrose Lightship	30	4 00 PM	12 00 N'n	5 40 PM
New York, Pier 52, N. R.	23	6 00 PM	2 00 PM	4 00 PM

Distance, Boston to New York, 305 miles.

New York, Pier 52, N. R.		4 00 PM	4 00 PM	7 00 AM
Scotland Lightship	21	5 50 PM	5 50 PM	4 10 AM
Highlands	4	6 10 PM	6 10 PM	4 00 AM
Barnegat Light	39	9 25 PM	9 25 PM	12 45 AM
Egg Harbor Light	20	10 50 PM	10 50 PM	10 55 PM
Absecon Light	12	11 50 PM	11 50 PM	9 55 PM
Five Fathom Bank Lightship	34	2 40 AM	2 40 AM	6 45 PM
Cape Hatteras Lightship	226 1/2	10 30 PM	10 30 PM	10 30 PM
Cape Lookout	70 1/2	4 45 AM	4 45 AM	4 15 PM
Fryingpan Lightship	82 1/2	11 45 AM	11 45 AM	9 15 AM
Martin's Industry Lightship	165	2 45 AM	2 45 AM	9 15 AM
Sea Buoy	11	3 45 AM	3 45 AM	6 15 PM
Savannah, Co.'s Wharf	24	6 00 AM	6 00 AM	4 00 PM

Distance, New York to Savannah, 710 miles.
Distances are in nautical miles of 6080.27 feet.

Savannah Line

BETWEEN
SAVANNAH, NEW YORK AND BOSTON.

POINTS OF INTEREST ALONG THE COAST.

CITY OF SAVANNAH

ROUTE: Savannah Line
PORTS: Boston, New York, Savannah
COMPANY: Ocean Steamship Co. of Savannah
OTHER NAMES: *LA GRANDE DUCHESSE, CAROLINA*

NUMBER: 141440
LENGTH: 380.0
BREADTH: 47.8
DRAUGHT: 16.5
GROSS TONNAGE: 5017.0

BUILT: 1896 - Newport News S. B. & D. D. Co., Newport News, Virginia.
HISTORY: Purchased, 1901, from Plant Line, formerly *LA GRANDE DUCHESSE*.
Purchased, 1905, by New York and Puerto Rico Line, then known as *CAROLINA*.
STATUS: Torpedoed, June 2, 1918.

CITY OF MACON

ROUTE:	Savannah Line	NUMBER:	127750
PORTS:	Boston, New York, Savannah	LENGTH:	377.5
COMPANY:	Ocean Steamship Co. of Savannah	BREADTH:	49.0
OTHER NAME:	*MACONA*	DRAUGHT:	15.8
		GROSS TONNAGE:	5311.0

BUILT: 1903 - Chester, Pennsylvania.

HISTORY: Conveyed by Ocean Steamship Co. of Savannah, Georgia, to Barber & Co., Inc., January 31, 1916.

STATUS: Wrecked off Sweden, January 17, 1920.

CITY OF ATLANTA

ROUTE:	Savannah Line	NUMBER:	201103
PORTS:	Boston, New York, Savannah	LENGTH:	377.5
COMPANY:	Ocean Steamship Co. of Savannah	BREADTH:	49.0
SISTER SHIP:	*CITY OF COLUMBUS*	DRAUGHT:	15.8
		GROSS TONNAGE:	5433.0

BUILT: 1904 - Chester, Pennsylvania.

HISTORY: Ran entire life on Savannah Line plus military service during World War II.

STATUS: Torpedoed in North West Atlantic, January 19, 1942, off Cape Hatteras. Forty-four lives lost, three saved.

CITY OF COLUMBUS

ROUTE: Savannah Line   NUMBER: 200840
PORTS: Boston, New York, Savannah   LENGTH: 337.5
COMPANY: Ocean Steamship Co. of Savannah   BREADTH: 49.0
SISTER SHIP: *CITY OF ATLANTA*   DRAUGHT: 15.8
                                                     GROSS TONNAGE: 5433.0

BUILT: 1904 - Chester, Pennsylvania.
HISTORY: Sold to Italy, 1934. (There was an earlier *CITY OF COLUMBUS* in 1878.)
STATUS: During World War II torpedoed with fatalities resulting.

CITY OF SAVANNAH (2)

ROUTE:	Savannah Line	NUMBER:	204437
PORTS:	Boston, New York, Savannah	LENGTH:	404.0
COMPANY:	Ocean Steamship Co. of Savannah	BREADTH:	49.0
		DRAUGHT:	23.0
		GROSS TONNAGE:	5654.0
		SPEED:	12 Knots

BUILT: 1907 - Delaware River Iron Shipbuilding Co., Chester, Pennsylvania.

HISTORY: Passenger accommodations removed for conversion to freighter, 1937. Converted to deep-sea type, 1942, with king post masts and new midship superstructure.

STATUS: Scrapped 1947.

CITY OF ATHENS

ROUTE:	Savannah Line		NUMBER:	208533
PORTS:	Boston, Savannah		LENGTH:	309.1
COMPANY:	Ocean Steamship Co. of Savannah		BREADTH:	46.2
OTHER NAME:	*SOMERSET*		DRAUGHT:	19.3
SISTER SHIP:	*CITY OF ROME*		GROSS TONNAGE:	3648.0

BUILT: 1911 - New York Shipbuilding and D. D. Co., Camden, New Jersey.

HISTORY: Sold by Merchants & Miners Steamship Co. to the Ocean Steamship Co. of Savannah, Georgia, October, 1917.

STATUS: May 1, 1918, collided with French cruiser *GLORIA* off Delaware Capes and sunk. Sixty-nine fatalities.

CITY OF ROME

ROUTE:	Savannah Line		NUMBER:	20838
PORTS:	Boston, Savannah		LENGTH:	309.
COMPANY:	Ocean Steamship Co. of Savannah		BREADTH:	46.
OTHER NAMES:	*SUWANNEE, VERAMAR, SOMERSET*		DRAUGHT:	19.
SISTER SHIP:	*CITY OF ATHENS*		GROSS TONNAGE:	3648.

BUILT: 1911 - New York Shipbuilding & D. D. Co., Camden, New Jersey.

HISTORY: Built for Merchants & Miners Co. originally. Sunk United States Submarine S-51 off Block Island Thirty-seven lives lost, three rescued, submarine sank immediately.

STATUS: Junked at Baltimore, Maryland, 1938.

CITY OF MONTGOMERY

ROUTE:	Savannah Line	NUMBER:	207362
PORTS:	Boston, New York, Savannah	LENGTH:	371.6
COMPANY:	Ocean Steamship Co. of Savannah	BREADTH:	49.7
SISTER SHIP:	*CITY OF ST. LOUIS*	DRAUGHT:	15.4
		GROSS TONNAGE:	5425.0

BUILT: 1910 - Newport News S. B. & D. D. Co., Newport News, Virginia.
STATUS: Scrapped 1948.

CITY OF ST. LOUIS

ROUTE:	Savannah Line	NUMBER:	207363
PORTS:	Boston, New York, Savannah	LENGTH:	371.4
COMPANY:	Ocean Steamship Co. of Savannah	BREADTH:	49.7
SISTER SHIP:	*CITY OF MONTGOMERY*	DRAUGHT:	15.4
		GROSS TONNAGE:	5425.0

BUILT: 1910 - Newport News S. B. & D. D. Co., Newport News, Virginia.
STATUS: Broken up, 1946.

Steamship Historical Society of America, Inc

CITY OF BIRMINGHAM

ROUTE:	Savannah Line	NUMBER:	223293
PORTS:	Boston, New York, Savannah	LENGTH:	381.8
COMPANY:	Ocean Steamship Co. of Savannah	BREADTH:	52.2
SISTER SHIP:	*CITY OF CHATTANOOGA*	DRAUGHT:	14.9
		GROSS TONNAGE:	5861.0

BUILT: 1923 - Newport News S. B. & D. D. Co., Newport News, Virginia.

STATUS: Sunk June 30, 1942.

CITY OF CHATTANOOGA

ROUTE:	Savannah Line	NUMBER:	223221
PORTS:	Boston, New York, Savannah	LENGTH:	381.8
COMPANY:	Ocean Steamship Co. of Savannah	BREADTH:	52.1
OTHER NAME:	*AMERICAN NAVIGATOR*	DRAUGHT:	14.9
SISTER SHIP:	*CITY OF BIRMINGHAM*	GROSS TONNAGE:	5861.0
BUILT:	1923 - Newport News S. B. & D. D. Co., Newport News, Virginia.		
STATUS:	Scrapped 1948.		

Chapter 15

Boston United Fruit Fleet

The Boston Fruit Company originated in 1885, eventually becoming the United Fruit Company (the Great White Fleet) March 30, 1899. Four men (three at first, and one later) were responsible for the United Fruit Company's prosperity in becoming the largest fruit growing corporation in the world.

Andrew E. Preston, a super banana salesman and banker, from Brookline and Beverly Farms, Massachusetts; Minor C. Keith, an excellent railroad builder and expert in the cultivation of bananas, came from New York; Captain L. B. Baker of Wellfleet, Massachusetts, a schooner owner and the originator of the idea to develop bananas commercially; and later Samuel Zemurray of the Cuyamel Company of New Orleans, headed the company in 1930 and made a number of expansions. These were the men responsible for the success of the company.

Elders and Fyffes Limited, of England, a competing fruit company supplying all of Europe, was acquired in 1910.

In 1914, the Revere Sugar Refinery was built in Charlestown, Massachusetts, and facilities were built in Cuba and Jamaica to ship the raw sugar in bulk to the refinery.

In December, 1929, the fleet of the Cuyamel Fruit Company was acquired.

Prior to 1922 all of the ships were coal burners. Between 1922 - 24 all had been converted to oil burners or diesels.

In addition to Boston, bananas were shipped from the Caribbean to New York City, Philadelphia, Baltimore, Charleston, Mobile, New Orleans and Galveston.

After using schooners for several years, the following four United States flagships were chartered: *ADMIRAL DEWEY, ADMIRAL FARRAGUT, ADMIRAL SAMPSON* and *ADMIRAL SCHLEY.*

Following this the company built its own fleet consisting of: *LIMON, ESPARTA, SAN JOSE* and later *ABANGAREZ, ZACAPA, SAN BLAS, SAN GIL, SAN BRUNO, SAN BENITO, LA PLAYA, LA MAREA, LA PERLA* and *CASTILLA.*

Later four sugar ships: *MACABI, MANAQUI, MARAVI* and *MAYARI* were built for the sugar trade.

Before World War II, the United Fruit Fleet in the American trade consisted of sixty ships. Elders and Fyffes Limited had thirty-one serving Great Britain and Europe. They also operated a tanker, making a total of ninety-two ships in the combined fleet.

The White Diamond, house flag and funnel insignia on a red background, was approved in June, 1901. The funnel was topped by a black band, then a white diamond, with the lower part of the stack painted buff.

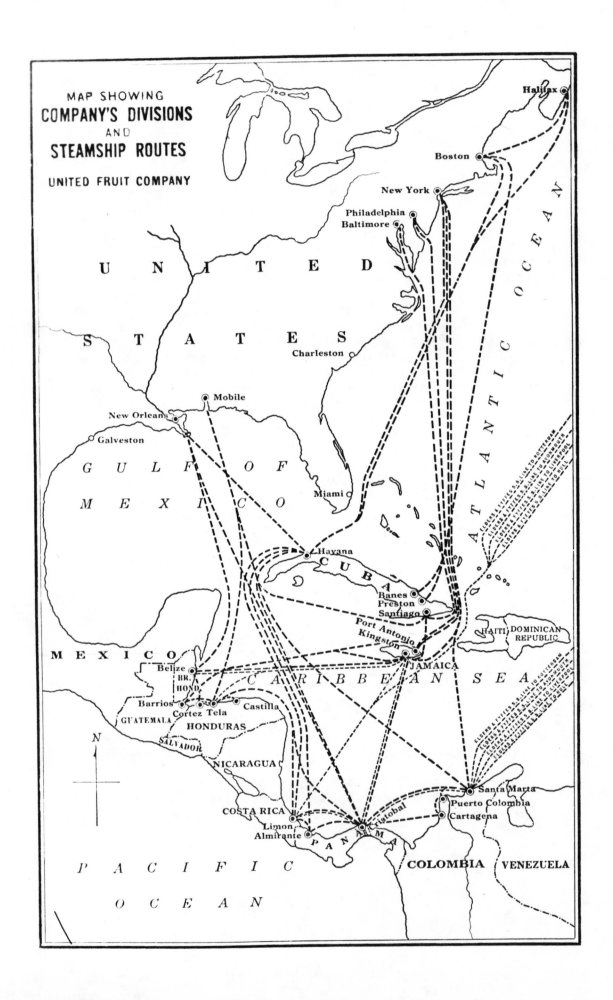

MAP SHOWING
COMPANY'S DIVISIONS
AND
STEAMSHIP ROUTES

UNITED FRUIT COMPANY

ADMIRAL DEWEY

ROUTE:	Chartered to the United Fruit Co.	NUMBER:	107417
PORTS:	Banana-loading ports in Guatemala,	LENGTH:	291.2
	Honduras, Costa Rica, Panama, Jamaica	BREADTH:	36.1
COMPANY:	American Mail Steamship Co., owners	DRAUGHT:	22.4
SISTER SHIPS:	*ADMIRAL FARRAGUT, ADMIRAL SAMPSON,*	GROSS TONNAGE:	1335.0
	ADMIRAL SCHLEY	SPEED:	12 Knots

LOCATION: Custom House Wharf, Boston, Massachusetts

BUILT: 1898 - Wm. Cramp & Sons, Co., Philadelphia, Pennsylvania.

HISTORY: In New York Harbor, Lower Bay, ran into the steamboat *MOUNT DESERT* and her starboard paddle box was carried away. Left United Fruit Company. Operated on West Coast to Alaska, 1913.

STATUS: Sold to Japan, 1935, for scrapping.

ADMIRAL FARRAGUT

ROUTE:	Chartered to the United Fruit Co.	NUMBER:	107423
PORTS:	Banana-loading ports in Guatemala,	LENGTH:	291.2
	Honduras, Costa Rica, Panama, Jamaica	BREADTH:	36.1
COMPANY:	American Mail Steamship Co., owners	DRAUGHT:	22.4
SISTER SHIPS:	*ADMIRAL DEWEY, ADMIRAL SAMPSON,*	GROSS TONNAGE:	1335.0
	ADMIRAL SCHLEY	SPEED:	12 Knots
LOCATION:	Backing away from a Boston pier.		
BUILT:	1898 - Wm. Cramp & Sons, Co., Philadelphia, Pennsylvania.		
HISTORY:	Owned by Pacific Steamship Line, 1925.		
	Left United Fruit Company, operated on West Coast to Alaska, 1913.		
STATUS:	Owned by Pacific Steamship Line, 1925.		

ADMIRAL SAMPSON

ROUTE:	Chartered to the United Fruit Co.	NUMBER:	107422
PORTS:	Banana-loading ports in Guatemala,	LENGTH:	291.2
	Honduras, Costa Rica, Panama, Jamaica	BREADTH:	36.1
COMPANY:	American Mail Steamship Co., owners	DRAUGHT:	22.4
SISTER SHIPS:	*ADMIRAL FARRAGUT, ADMIRAL DEWEY*	GROSS TONNAGE:	1335.0
	ADMIRAL SCHLEY	SPEED:	12 Knots
LOCATION:	Boston Harbor		
BUILT:	1898 - Wm. Cramp & Sons, Co., Philadelphia, Pennsylvania.		
HISTORY:	Left United Fruit Company, operated on West Coast to Alaska, 1913.		
	Sold 1918 to Pacific Steamship Co.		

ADMIRAL SCHLEY

ROUTE:	Chartered to the United Fruit Co.	NUMBER:	107422
PORTS:	Banana-loading ports in Guatemala,	LENGTH:	291.2
	Honduras, Costa Rica, Panana, Jamaica	BREADTH:	36.1
COMPANY:	American Mail Steamship Co., owners	DRAUGHT:	22.4
SISTER SHIPS:	*ADMIRAL FARRAGUT, ADMIRAL DEWEY*	GROSS TONNAGE:	1335.0
	ADMIRAL SAMPSON	SPEED:	12.5 Knots
LOCATION:	Custom House Wharf, Boston, Massachusetts		
BUILT:	1898 - Wm. Cramp & Sons, Co., Philadelphia, Pennsylvania.		
HISTORY:	Left United Fruit Company, operated on West Coast to Alaska, 1913. Sold 1918 to Pacific Steamship Co.		
STATUS:	Sold to Japan for scrapping, 1934.		

LIMON (American Flag)

ROUTE:	Caribbean Service	NUMBER:	212592
PORTS:	In Guatemala, Honduras, Costa Rica,	LENGTH:	330.6
	Panama, Jamaica	BREADTH:	44.5
COMPANY:	United Fruit Co.	DRAUGHT:	13.9
SISTER SHIPS:	*ESPARTA, SAN JOSE*	GROSS TONNAGE:	3266.0
LOCATION:	Boston Harbor	SPEED:	12.5 Knots
BUILT:	1904 - Workman, Clark, & Co. Ltd., Belfast, Ireland.		
STATUS:	Grounded on a coral reef, July 24, 1938. Due to extensive damage, sold for scrap to Boston Iron & Metal Company, Baltimore, Maryland, December 13, 1938.		

ESPARTA (American Flag)

ROUTE:	Caribbean Service	NUMBER:	212606
PORTS:	In Guatemala, Honduras, Costa Rica,	LENGTH:	330.6
	Panama, Jamaica	BREADTH:	44.6
COMPANY:	United Fruit Co.	DRAUGHT:	13.9
SISTER SHIPS:	*LIMON, SAN JOSE*	GROSS TONNAGE:	3365.0
LOCATION:	Boston Harbor	SPEED:	12.5 Knots
BUILT:	1904 - Workman, CLark & Co. Ltd., Belfast, Ireland.		
STATUS:	Torpedoed and sunk off Jacksonville, Florida, 1:15 a.m., April 9, 1942.		

Steamship Historical Society of America, Inc.

SAN JOSE (American Flag)

ROUTE:	Caribbean Service	NUMBER:	212635
PORTS:	In Guatemala, Honduras, Costa Rica,	LENGTH:	330.5
	Panama, Jamaica	BREADTH:	44.6
COMPANY:	United Fruit Co.	DRAUGHT:	13.9
SISTER SHIPS:	LIMON, ESPARTA	GROSS TONNAGE:	3358.0
LOCATION:	Sailing out of Boston Harbor	SPEED:	12.5 Knots.
BUILT:	1904 - Workman, Clark, & Co. Ltd., Belfast, Ireland.		
STATUS:	Due to wartime black-out conditions, collided with Grace Line vessel, SANTA ELISA. Sunk about twelve miles south of Atlantic City, New Jersey, January 7, 1942.		

ABANGAREZ (American Flag)

ROUTE:	Caribbean Service	NUMBER:	212612
PORTS:	In Guatemala, Honduras, Costa Rica,	LENGTH:	378.8
	Panama, Jamaica	BREADTH:	50.3
COMPANY:	United Fruit Co.	DRAUGHT:	29.1
SISTER SHIPS:	*ZACAPA, TURRIALBA, ATENAS,*	GROSS TONNAGE:	4538.0
	ALMIRANTE, SANTA MARTA, and *METAPAN*		
BUILT:	1909 - Workman, Clark & Co. Ltd., Belfast, Ireland.		
STATUS:	Traded to United States Maritime Commission, February 6, 1946.		

ZACAPA (American Flag)

OUTE:	Caribbean Service	NUMBER:	212583
ORTS:	In Guatemala, Honduras, Costa Rica,	LENGTH:	378.9
	Panama, Jamica	BREADTH:	50.3
OMPANY:	United Fruit Co.	DRAUGHT:	29.1
STER SHIPS:	*ABANGAREZ, TURRIALBA, ATENAS,*	GROSS TONNAGE:	4736.0
	ALMIRANTE, SANTA MARTA, and *METAPAN*	SPEED:	14 Knots
UILT:	1909 - Workman, CLark & Co. Ltd., Belfast, Ireland.		
STORY:	Traded to United States Maritime Commission, December 13, 1945.		
TATUS:	Dismantled at Bordentown, New Jersey, 1954.		

SAN PABLO (Panamanian Flag)

ROUTE:	Caribbean Service	NUMBER:	HPC
PORTS:	In Guatemala, Honduras, Costa Rica, Panama, Jamaica	LENGTH:	315.
		BREADTH:	44.
COMPANY:	Balboa Shipping Co., Inc. (United Fruit Co.)	DRAUGHT:	28.
		GROSS TONNAGE:	3305.
BUILT:	1915 - Workman, Clark & Co. Ltd., Belfast, Ireland.		
STATUS:	Torpedoed while docked at Limon, Costa Rica, July 2, 1942. Raised and later towed to a Unite States port. Declared total loss.		

326

SAN BLAS (Panamanian Flag)

ROUTE:	Caribbean Service		NUMBER:	144209
PORTS:	In Guatemala, Honduras, Costa Rica,		LENGTH:	325.0
	Panama, Jamaica		BREADTH:	46.3
COMPANY:	Balboa Shipping Co, Inc.		DRAUGHT:	29.2
	(United Fruit Co.)		GROSS TONNAGE:	3628.0
SISTER SHIPS:	*SAN BENITO, SAN BRUNO, SAN GIL*			
LOCATION:	Boston Harbor			
BUILT:	1920 - Workman, Clark & Co. Ltd., Belfast, Ireland.			
STATUS:	Torpedoed and sunk June 16, 1942. Position: 25° 26′ North 95° 35′ West.			

SAN GIL (Panamanian Flag)

ROUTE: Caribbean Service

PORTS: In Guatemala, Honduras, Costa Rica, Panama, Jamaica

COMPANY: Balboa Shipping Co., Inc. (United Fruit Co.)

SISTER SHIPS: *SAN BENITO, SAN BRUNO, SAN BLAS*

LOCATION: Boston Harbor

BUILT: 1920 - Workman, Clark & Co. Ltd., Belfast, Ireland.

STATUS: Torpedoed 11:50 p.m., February 3, 1942, and sunk off Chincoteague Inlet (between Cape May and Cape Charles).

NUMBER: HPCC

LENGTH: 325.0

BREADTH: 46.3

DRAUGHT: 29.2

GROSS TONNAGE: 3627.0

SAN BRUNO (Panamanian Flag)

ROUTE:	Caribbean Service	NUMBER:	HPCA
PORTS:	In Guatemala, Honduras, Costa Rica,	LENGTH:	325.0
	Panama, Jamaica	BREADTH:	46.3
COMPANY:	Balboa Shipping Co., Inc.	DRAUGHT:	29.2
	(United Fruit Co.)	GROSS TONNAGE:	3627.0
SISTER SHIPS:	SAN BLAS, SAN GIL, SAN BENITO		
LOCATION:	Boston Harbor		
BUILT:	1920 - Workman, Clark & Co. Ltd., Belfast, Ireland.		
HISTORY:	Sold May 22, 1947.		

SAN BENITO (Panamanian & Honduran Flags)

ROUTE:	Caribbean Service	NUMBER:	144219
PORTS:	In Guatemala, Honduras, Costa Rica, Panama, Jamaica	LENGTH:	325.3
		BREADTH:	46.3
COMPANY:	Balboa Shipping Co., Inc. (United Fruit Co.)	DRAUGHT:	29.2
		GROSS TONNAGE:	3724.0
OTHER NAME:	TAURUS (during Navy service)		
SISTER SHIPS:	SAN BRUNO, SAN BLAS, SAN GIL		
LOCATION:	Boston Harbor		
BUILT:	1921 - Workman, Clark & Co. Ltd., Belfast, Ireland.		
STATUS:	Sold to Pinto Island Metals Company for scrap January 15, 1953.		

LA PLAYA (Panamanian & Honduran Flags)

ROUTE:	Caribbean Service	NUMBER:	HPAM
PORTS:	In Guatemala, Honduras, Costa Rica,	LENGTH:	325.2
	Panama, Jamaica	BREADTH:	48.1
COMPANY:	Balboa Shipping Co., Inc.	DRAUGHT:	28.3
	(United Fruit Co.)	GROSS TONNAGE:	3628.0
BUILT:	1923 - Cammell, Laird & Co. Ltd., Birkenhead, England.		
HISTORY:	Sold to John S. Latsis, Athens, Greece, May 21, 1964.		

Steamship Historical Society of America, Inc

LA MAREA (Panamanian & Honduran Flags)

ROUTE:	Caribbean Service	NUMBER:	HPBD
PORTS:	In Guatemala, Honduras, Costa Rica	LENGTH:	352.
	Panama, Jamaica	BREADTH:	48.
COMPANY:	Balboa Shipping Co., Inc.	DRAUGHT:	28.
	(United Fruit Co.)	GROSS TONNAGE:	4281.0
OTHER NAME:	DARIEN		
LOCATION:	Custom House Wharf, Boston, Massachusetts		
BUILT:	1924 - Cammell, Laird & Co. Ltd., Birkenhead, England.		
STATUS:	Sold to Bethlehem Steel for scrap, July 23, 1954.		

Mariners Museum, Newport News, Virginia

LA PERLA (American Flag)

ROUTE:	Caribbean Service	NUMBER:	225181
PORTS:	In Guatemala, Honduras, Costa Rica,	LENGTH:	325.2
	Panama, Jamaica	BREADTH:	48.1
COMPANY:	United Fruit Steamship Corp.	DRAUGHT:	28.3
OTHER NAME:	*U.S.S. CYGNET* (during Navy service)	GROSS TONNAGE:	3792.0
LOCATION:	Boston Harbor		
BUILT:	1925 - Cammell , Laird & Co. Ltd., Birkenhead, England.		
HISTORY:	Sold to Caribbean Land and Shipping Company, January 23, 1947.		

CASTILLA (Honduran Flag)

ROUTE:	Caribbean Service	NUMBER:	HRAH
PORTS:	In Guatemala, Honduras, Costa Rica,	LENGTH:	341.9
	Panama, Jamaica	BREADTH:	48.0
COMPANY:	United Fruit Co.	DRAUGHT:	28.2
LOCATION:	Custom House Wharf, Boston, Massachusetts	GROSS TONNAGE:	4087.0
BUILT:	1927 - Workman, Clark & Co. Ltd., Belfast, Ireland.		
STATUS:	Torpedoed and sunk June 6, 1942, at 8:50 p.m. Position: 20° 15' North 83° 18' West.		

MACABI (Panamanian Flag)

ROUTE:	Boston - Cuba - Jamaica	NUMBER:	144251
PORTS:	Boston, Preston, Port Antonio	LENGTH:	303.0
COMPANY:	Balboa Shipping Co., Inc.	BREADTH:	47.2
	(United Fruit Co.)	DRAUGHT:	21.5
SISTER SHIPS:	MANAQUI, MARAVI, MAYARI	GROSS TONNAGE:	2802.0
LOCATION:	Boston Harbor		
BUILT:	1921 - Workman, Clark & Co. Ltd., Belfast, Ireland.		
HISTORY:	Ran in company service supplying Revere Sugar Refinery, Boston, with raw sugar from Cuba and Jamaica.		

Mariners Museum, Newport News, Virginia

MANAQUI (Panamanian Flag)

ROUTE:	Boston - Cuba - Jamaica	NUMBER:	91228
PORTS:	Boston, Preston, Port Antonio	LENGTH:	303.0
COMPANY:	Balboa Shipping Co., Inc.	BREADTH:	47.2
	(United Fruit Co.)	DRAUGHT:	21.7
SISTER SHIPS:	MACABI, MARAVI, MAYARI	GROSS TONNAGE:	2802.0
LOCATION:	Boston Harbor		
BUILT:	1921 - Workman, Clark & Co. Ltd., Belfast, Ireland.		
HISTORY:	Sold to Furness, Withy & Co. Ltd., 1937. While owned by United Fruit Company, ran in company service supplying Revere Sugar Refinery, Boston, with raw sugar from Cuba and Jamaica.		

336

MARAVI (Panamanian Flag)

ROUTE:	Boston - Cuba - Jamaica	NUMBER:	144257
PORTS:	Boston, Preston, Port Antonio	LENGTH:	303.0
COMPANY:	Balboa Shipping Co., Inc.	BREADTH:	46.2
	(United Fruit Co.)	DRAUGHT:	21.7
OTHER NAME:	*JANE LANNG*	GROSS TONNAGE:	2802.0
SISTER SHIPS:	*MANAQUI, MAYARI, MACABI*		
LOCATION:	Boston Harbor		
BUILT:	1921 - Workman, Clark & Co. Ltd., Belfast, Ireland.		
HISTORY:	Ran in company service supplying Revere Sugar Refinery, Boston, with raw sugar from Cuba and Jamaica.		

MAYARI (Panamanian Flag)

ROUTE:	Boston - Cuba - Jamaica	NUMBER:	144247
PORTS:	Boston, Preston, Port Antonio	LENGTH:	303.0
COMPANY:	Balboa Shipping Co., Inc.	BREADTH:	47.2
	(United Fruit Co.)	DRAUGHT:	21.7
SISTER SHIPS:	MANAQUI, MARAVI, MACABI	GROSS TONNAGE:	2802.0
BUILT:	1921 - Workman, Clark & Co. Ltd., Belfast, Ireland.		
HISTORY:	Ran in company service supplying Revere Sugar Refinery, Boston, with raw sugar from Cuba and Jamaica.		

Chapter 16

Canadian National "Lady Ships"

Between World Wars I and II, the Canadian National operated: *LADY DRAKE,*
LADY HAWKINS, LADY NELSON, LADY RODNEY and *LADY SOMERS.*

Summer ports of call were: Montreal, Halifax, Boston, Hamilton (Bermuda),
Barbados, Antigua, Dominica, St. Lucia, St. Vincent, Granada, Trinidad,
Georgetown and British Guyana.

These steamers operating from Halifax called at Nassau, the Bahamas,
during the winter.

The first *LADY* ship to sail to the West Indies was *LADY SOMERS*, leaving
Halifax, April 12, 1929, for Bermuda, Nassau and Jamaica.

LADY NELSON and *LADY RODNEY* were the last of the steamers in service
when it terminated October 25, 1952.

LADY DRAKE (British)

ROUTE:	Halifax, Nova Scotia - Boston - West Indies	NUMBER:	155050
PORTS:	Montreal, Halifax, Boston, Hamilton (Bermuda),	LENGTH:	419.5
	Barbados, Antigua, Dominica, St. Lucia, St. Vincent,	BREADTH:	55.1
	Grenada, Trinidad, Georgetown, British Guyana	DRAUGHT:	28.2
COMPANY:	Canadian National Railroad Co.	GROSS TONNAGE:	7846.0
SISTER SHIPS:	*LADY HAWKINS, LADY NELSON*		
LOCATION:	Boston Harbor		
BUILT:	1928 - Cammell, Laird Co. Ltd., Birkenhead, England.		
STATUS:	Torpedoed, May 5, 1942.		

LADY HAWKINS (British)

ROUTE:	Halifax, Nova Scotia - Boston - West Indies	NUMBER:	155047
PORTS:	Montreal, Halifax, Boston, Hamilton (Bermuda),	LENGTH:	419.5
	Barbados, Antigua, Dominica, St. Lucia, St. Vincent,	BREADTH:	55.1
	Grenada, Trinidad, Georgetown, British Guyana	DRAUGHT:	28.2
COMPANY:	Canadian National Railroad Co.	GROSS TONNAGE:	7846.0
SISTER SHIPS:	LADY DRAKE, LADY NELSON		
LOCATION:	Boston Harbor		
BUILT:	1928 - Cammell, Laird Co. Ltd., Birkenhead, England.		
STATUS:	Torpedoed, January 19, 1942, 1:50 a.m. 250 fatalities, seventy-one survived.		

LADY NELSON (British)

ROUTE:	Halifax, Nova Scotia - Boston - West Indies	NUMBER:	15504
PORTS:	Montreal, Halifax, Boston, Hamilton (Bermuda),	LENGTH:	419.
	Barbados, Antigua, Dominica, St. Lucia, St. Vincent,	BREADTH:	55.
	Grenada, Trinidad, Georgetown, British Guyana	DRAUGHT:	28.
COMPANY:	Canadian National Railroad Co.	GROSS TONNAGE:	7831.
OTHER NAME:	*GUMHURYAT*		
SISTER SHIPS:	*LADY DRAKE, LADY HAWKINS*		
BUILT:	1928 - Cammell. Laird Co. Ltd., Birkenhead, England.		
HISTORY:	Last trip from Boston, September 27, 1952. Sold 1953 to Khedivial Mail Line, Alexandria, Egyp		
	This ship and *LADY RODNEY* were the last in the service, which terminated October 25, 1952.		
STATUS:	Torpedoed by Submarine, St. Lucia, West Indies. Saved and repaired.		

LADY RODNEY (British)

ROUTE:	Halifax, Nova Scotia - Boston - West Indies		NUMBER:	154460
PORTS:	Montreal, Halifax, Boston, Hamilton (Bermuda),		LENGTH:	420.5
	Barbados, Antigua, Dominica, St. Lucia, St. Vincent,		BREADTH:	60.2
	Grenada, Trinidad, Georgetown, British Guyana		DRAUGHT:	30.2
COMPANY:	Canadian National Railroad Co.		GROSS TONNAGE:	8194.0
OTHER NAME:	*MECCA*			
SISTER SHIP:	*LADY SOMERS*			
LOCATION:	Boston Harbor			
BUILT:	1929 - Cammell. Laird Co. Ltd., Birkenhead, England.			
HISTORY:	Last sailing from Boston, October 30, 1952. This ship and the *LADY NELSON* were the last in the service, which terminated October 25, 1952.			
STATUS:	Sold 1953 to Khedivial Mail Line, Alexandria, Egypt.			

LADY SOMERS (British)

ROUTE:	Halifax, Nova Scotia - Boston - West Indies	NUMBER:	154459
PORTS:	Montreal, Halifax, Boston, Hamilton (Bermuda),	LENGTH:	420.0
	Barbados, Antigua, Dominica, St. Lucia, St. Vincent,	BREADTH:	60.2
	Grenada, Trinidad, Georgetown, British Guyana	DRAUGHT:	30.2
COMPANY:	Canadian National Railroad Co.	GROSS TONNAGE:	8194.0
SISTER SHIP:	LADY RODNEY		
LOCATION:	Boston Harbor		
BUILT:	1929 - Cammell, Laird Co. Ltd., Birkenhead, England.		
HISTORY:	Left Halifax on first trip to Bermuda, Nassau, and Jamaica April 12, 1929.		

Chapter 17

Nantucket and Martha's Vineyard Vessels

The *EAGLE'S WING*, one of the first steamboats in New England, ran from New Bedford to Nantucket and way landings. In competition with the *EAGLE'S WING* was another early steamboat, the *METACOMET*.

The *MONOHANSETT* ran from Edgartown to Fair Haven. The *RIVER QUEEN* ran between Providence and Martha's Vineyard. The *ISLAND HOME* ran between Nantucket and Hyannis.

The following vessels: *MARTHA'S VINEYARD, NANTUCKET, GAY HEAD, UNCATENA, SANKATY, MARTHA'S VINEYARD* (2), *NANTUCKET* (2), *NEW BEDFORD* and *NAUSHON* were operated by the New Bedford, Martha's Vineyard and Nantucket Steamboat Company.

Owned by the New Haven Railroad, this subsidiary maintained high earnings showing the best record of any of the New Haven properties for several years. Under this ownership excellent service was provided with the most modern equipment being used. Following this company, the service was provided by a Commonwealth of Massachusetts line.

EAGLE'S WING

ROUTE: New Bedford - Nantucket

PORTS: New Bedford, Fairhaven, Woods Hole, Edgartown, Nantucket

COMPANY: New Bedford & Nantucket Steamboat Co.

OTHER NAME: *YOUNG AMERICA*

NUMBER: *

LENGTH: 173.0

BREADTH: 27.0

DRAUGHT: 9.0

GROSS TONNAGE: 409.6

* Official numbering did not begin until 1867.

BUILT: 1854 - Sneeden & Whitlock, Greenpoint, New York.

STATUS: Caught fire and burned, July 24, 1861, while on excursion trip out of Providence, proceeding up Providence River racing with *PERRY*. All lives saved by going overboard.

METACOMET

ROUTE: Edgartown - Fairhaven
PORTS: Edgartown, Fairhaven

NUMBER: *
LENGTH: 119.0
BREADTH: 26.0
DRAUGHT: 10.0
GROSS TONNAGE: 395.0

* Official numbering did not begin until 1867.

BUILT: 1854 - New York, New York.

HISTORY: 1857, sold to United States Government as gunboat *PULASKI*. 1863, sold at Montevideo and used on River Platte.

MONOHANSETT

ROUTE:	New Bedford - Nantucket Line	NUMBER:	16795
PORTS:	New Bedford, Woods Hole, Oak Bluffs, Nantucket	LENGTH:	174.8
COMPANY:	New Bedford, Martha's Vineyard &	BREADTH:	28.2
	Nantucket Steamboat Co.	DRAUGHT:	9.6
		GROSS TONNAGE:	489.0
BUILT:	1862 - New York, New York.		
STATUS:	Ran ashore in thick fog near Misery Islands, Boston, Massachusetts, August 3, 1904. Total loss		

RIVER QUEEN

ROUTE:	Providence - Martha's Vineyard	NUMBER:	21455
PORTS:	Providence, Martha's Vineyard	LENGTH:	181.1
COMPANY:	Vineyard Co., chartered to	BREADTH:	28.5
	Old Colony Railroad Co.	DRAUGHT:	9.0
LOCATION:	Oak Bluffs, Martha's Vineyard, Massachusetts, 1864	GROSS TONNAGE:	578.37
BUILT:	1864 - Keyport, New Jersey.		
HISTORY:	1873-1881, with *ISLAND HOME* as replacement for *MONOHANSETT*.		
STATUS:	Burned July 9, 1911, Washington, D.C.		

ISLAND HOME

ROUTE:	Nantucket - Hyannis	NUMBER:	12141
PORTS:	Nantucket, Hyannis	LENGTH:	184.0
COMPANY:	Nantucket & Cape Cod Steamboat Co.	BREADTH:	29.6
		DRAUGHT:	11.0
		GROSS TONNAGE:	484.0

BUILT: 1855 - Greenpoint, New York.
HISTORY: At Nantucket 1884. Sold 1895 and converted to barge.

MARTHA'S VINEYARD

ROUTE: Nantucket Line
PORTS: New Bedford, Woods Hole, Oak Bluffs, Nantucket
COMPANY: New Bedford, Martha's Vineyard &
Nantucket Steamboat Co.
OTHER NAME: *KEYPORT*
BUILT: 1871 - Brooklyn, New York.
HISTORY: Renamed *KEYPORT*, May 23, 1913.
STATUS: July 22, 1916, struck by a Lighter at the Battery, New York City. Raised July 24, 1916. Never ran again.

NUMBER: 90288
LENGTH: 171.2
BREADTH: 28.0
DRAUGHT: 9.4
GROSS TONNAGE: 515.0

NANTUCKET

ROUTE:	Nantucket Line	NUMBER:	130354
PORTS:	New Bedford, Woods Hole, Oak Bluffs, Nantucket	LENGTH:	190.0
COMPANY:	New Bedford, Martha's Vineyard &	BREADTH:	33.0
	Nantucket Steamboat Co.	DRAUGHT:	9.0
OTHER NAME:	*POINT COMFORT*	GROSS TONNAGE:	629.0
		SPEED:	15 Knots

BUILT: 1886 - Camden, New Jersey.

HISTORY: Sold to Keansburg Steamboat Company, June 19, 1913.

STATUS: Stranded on Esopus Island, New York, September 17, 1919.

GAY HEAD

ROUTE:	Nantucket Line	NUMBER:	86151
PORTS:	New Bedford, Martha's Vineyard, Nantucket	LENGTH:	203.0
COMPANY:	New Bedford, Martha's Vineyard &	BREADTH:	34.0
	Nantucket Steamboat Co.	DRAUGHT:	11.6
OTHER NAME:	*PASTIME*	GROSS TONNAGE:	701.0
BUILT:	1891 - Philadelphia, Pennsylvania.		
HISTORY:	Renamed *PASTIME* at New York City, June 21, 1924.		
STATUS:	Burned for old metal, October 20, 1931. Abandoned June 30, 1932.		

UNCATENA

ROUTE:	Nantucket Line	NUMBER:	25351
PORTS:	New Bedford, Woods Hole, Oak Bluffs, Nantucket	LENGTH:	178.0
COMPANY:	New Bedford, Martha's Vineyard &	BREADTH:	31.0
	Nantucket Steamboat Co.	DRAUGHT:	12.0
OTHER NAME:	*PEMBERTON*	GROSS TONNAGE:	652.0
BUILT:	1902 - Pusey & Jones Co., Wilmington, Delaware.		
HISTORY:	Sold to Nantasket Steamboat Company after Thanksgiving Day fire. Renamed *PEMBERTON*. A forward deck was added.		
STATUS:	Scrapped at Quincy, Massachusetts, 1937.		

R. Loren Graham

SANKATY

ROUTE:	Nantucket Line	NUMBER:	208399
PORTS:	New Bedford, Woods Hole, Oak Bluffs, Nantucket	LENGTH:	1871.5
COMPANY:	New England Steamship Co.	BREADTH:	38.2
	(New Haven Railroad)	DRAUGHT:	11.3
OTHER NAME:	(Canadian) *CHARLES A. DUNNING*	GROSS TONNAGE:	342.0

BUILT: 1911 - Fore River Shipbuilding Co., Quincy Massachusetts.

HISTORY: Sold to Northumberland Ferries Ltd., Charlottetown, Prince Edward Island, Canada, February, 1940. Ran season of 1953.

STATUS: *CHARLES A DUNNING* did not run 1964. Scrapped, Pictou, Nova Scotia, August, 1964.

MARTHA'S VINEYARD (2)

ROUTE:	Nantucket Line	NUMBER:	223089
PORTS:	New Bedford, Woods Hole, Oak Bluffs, Nantucket	LENGTH:	202.4
COMPANY:	New England Steamship Co. (New Haven Railroad)	BREADTH:	36.1
		DRAUGHT:	13.1
OTHER NAME:	*ISLANDER*	GROSS TONNAGE:	1089.0
SISTER SHIPS	*NEW BEDFORD, NANTUCKET* (2)		
BUILT:	1923 - Bath Iron Works, Inc., Bath, Maine.		
HISTORY:	Renamed *MARTHA'S VINEYARD* in 1928. Owned by Island Steamship Lines, Inc., January, 1948. Boston - Providence Line, 1961.		
STATUS:	Running 1977.		

R. Loren Graham

NANTUCKET (3)

ROUTE:	Nantucket Line	NUMBER:	224501
PORTS:	New Bedford, Woods Hole, Oak Bluffs, Nantucket	LENGTH:	202.4
COMPANY:	New England Steamship Co.	BREADTH:	35.1
	(New Haven Railroad)	DRAUGHT:	13.1
OTHER NAMES:	NOBSKA	GROSS TONNAGE:	1082.0
SISTER SHIPS:	MARTHA'S VINEYARD (2), NEW BEDFORD		
BUILT:	1925 - Bath Iron Works, Inc., Bath, Maine.		
HISTORY:	Sold to Massachusetts Steamship Lines, Inc., December 31, 1945. 1968, called NOBSKA.		

NEW BEDFORD

ROUTE:	Nantucket Line	NUMBER:	227565
PORTS:	New Bedford, Woods Hole, Oak Bluffs, Nantucket	LENGTH:	202.6
COMPANY:	New England Steamship Co.	BREADTH:	36.2
	(New Haven Railroad)	DRAUGHT:	13.0
SISTER SHIPS	*NANTUCKET* (2), *MARTHA'S VINEYARD* (2)	GROSS TONNAGE:	1116.0
BUILT:	1928 - Bethlehem Shipbuilding Corp., Quincy, Massachusetts. Ran on Providence - Block Island Line, 1951. Witte Marine Equipment Co., Inc., 1968.		
STATUS:	Running, 1979.		

R. Loren Graham

NAUSHON

ROUTE: Nantucket Line
PORTS: New Bedford, Woods Hole, Oak Bluffs, Nantucket
COMPANY: New England Steamship Co.
(New Haven Railroad)
OTHER NAME: *JOHN A. MESECK*
BUILT: 1929 - Bethlehem Shipbuilding Corp., Quincy, Massachusetts.
HISTORY: Requisitioned by United States Navy, 1942.
Renamed *JOHN A. MESECK*, April 28, 1947.
STATUS: A Union School ship at Norfolk, Virginia, 1968.

NUMBER: 228581
LENGTH: 240.0
BREADTH: 45.2
DRAUGHT: 14.0
GROSS TONNAGE: 1978.0

Chapter 18

Cuttyhunk Vessels

The following vessels: *HELEN AUGUSTA, CYGNET, GOSNOLD, FRANCES* (2) and *ALERT* were owned by various groups and ran at different periods. The *ALERT* is believed to be still operating.

Carrying freight, mail, and passengers, these vessels ran from New Bedford to Cuttyhunk Island.

Cuttyhunk Island is the outermost of the Elizabeth Islands in Buzzard's Bay, fifteen miles off the coast from New Bedford, Massachusetts.

In 1602 the English explorer, Bartholomew Gosnold, with thirty-two comrades, settled on Cuttyhunk Island, establishing the first English colony in New England.

Gosnold is the corporate name of the Elizabeth Islands.

Some of the islands comprising the group are Uncatena, Monohansett, Naushon and Nashawena.

Three of the islands are privately owned by the Forbes family of Boston.

HELEN AUGUSTA

ROUTE:	Cuttyhunk Line	NUMBER:	11331
PORTS:	New Bedford, Cuttyhunk	LENGTH:	82.7
COMPANY:	Vineyard Steamboat Co.	BREADTH:	21.2
OTHER NAME:	*JOSEFA CROSBY*	DRAUGHT:	6.5
LOCATION:	Cuttyhunk Dock	GROSS TONNAGE:	132.0
BUILT:	1863 - Clinton, New York.		
HISTORY:	Cuttyhunk Line, 1874-1876.		
STATUS:	Abandoned, 1879.		

CYGNET

ROUTE:	Cuttyhunk Line	NUMBER:	12551
PORTS:	New Bedford, Cuttyhunk	LENGTH:	62
		BREADTH:	16
		DRAUGHT:	6
		GROSS TONNAGE:	43

BUILT: 1876 - Noank, Connecticut.
HISTORY: Cuttyhunk Line, 1885-1905.
STATUS: Destroyed by fire at Shadyside, New Jersey, December 20, 1917.

R. Loren Graham

GOSNOLD

ROUTE:	Cuttyhunk Line	NUMBER:	203183
PORTS:	New Bedford, Cuttyhunk	LENGTH:	103.0
OTHER NAMES:	*MIRAMAR, W. S. WHITE, CARIBBEAN*	BREADTH:	24.3
LOCATION:	Palmer's Island Light,	DRAUGHT:	9.4
	New Bedford, Massachusetts	GROSS TONNAGE:	181.0
		SPEED:	13 Knots

BUILT: 1906 - Noank, Connecticut.

HISTORY: Cuttyhunk Line, 1906-1917.
United States Army, 1917-1921.
New York area, 1921-1934.
Rockland - Vinalhaven, Maine, 1934-1942, *W. S. WHITE*.
Port of Spain, Trinidad.

STATUS: Burned in Trinidad.

FRANCES (2)

ROUTE: Cuttyhunk Line
PORTS: New Bedford, Cuttyhunk

BUILT: 1914 - Boothbay Harbor, Maine.
HISTORY: Cuttyhunk Line, 1918-1922.
                  Sold to Bermuda, 1923.

NUMBER: 212026
LENGTH: 57.9
BREADTH: 20.2
DRAUGHT: 6.3
GROSS TONNAGE: 56.0

C. Bradford Mitchell

ALERT

ROUTE: Cuttyhunk Line
PORTS: New Bedford, Cuttyhunk
COMPANY: New Bedford Tugboat Co., Inc.
LOCATION: Her Pier in New Bedford, Massachusetts

BUILT: 1917 - Wareham, Massachusetts.
HISTORY: Cuttyhunk Line, 1923 to present date.
STATUS: Still operating, 1980.

NUMBER: 215337
LENGTH: 56.7
BREADTH: 17.2
DRAUGHT: 7.8
GROSS TONNAGE: 43.0

Chapter 19

Narragansett and Mount Hope Bay Vessels

In all of New England the Providence River, Narragansett Bay and Mount Hope Bay area seems to have been the most popular region for steamboat excursions. In the late 1800's it was not uncommon for fifty thousand excursionists to spend Sundays and holidays on the rivers and bays.

As early as 1817 regular steamboat service was provided between Providence and Newport. Year-round steamboat service connected Fall River, Bristol and Providence from 1827.

Many of the steamers in this group were previously shown in other areas of New England. Due to their popularity in the Providence area they are repeated in this chapter as follows: *AWASHONKS, MONHEGAN, MAY ARCHER, SPRIGG CARROLL, PEMAQUID, WESTPORT, BLOCK ISLAND (2) (MACHIGONNE)* and *CHAUNCEY M. DEPEW (RANGELEY)*. Although the *SAPPHO* serviced the Providence area for several years a photograph could not be located.

RADFORD DURFEE

		NUMBER:	2172
TE:	Fall River - Providence	LENGTH:	154.5
TS:	Fall River, Providence	BREADTH:	25.3
		DRAUGHT:	9.0
		GROSS TONNAGE:	333.1

LT: 1845 - Lawrence & Sneeden, New York, New York.

TORY: Burned and sank January 25, 1864, at Fall River, Massachusetts. Raised and used January 30, 1864.

TUS: Abandoned, broken up, 1884, at Mt. Hope Bay.

RIVER BELLE

ROUTE:	Providence Harbor	NUMBER:	149
OTHER NAMES:	*CRICKET, L. BOARDMAN*	LENGTH:	138
LOCATION:	Providence, Rhode Island, Dock	BREADTH:	21
		DRAUGHT:	7
		GROSS TONNAGE:	121

BUILT:	1846 - New York, New York.
HISTORY:	Name changed to *RIVER BELLE*, April 3, 1880.
STATUS:	Beached at Weehawken Basin, October 4, 1894.

CANONICUS

ROUTE:	Fall River - Providence	NUMBER:	4433
PORTS:	Fall River, Newport, Providence	LENGTH:	178.3
COMPANY:	Fall River & Providence Steamboat Co.	BREADTH:	28.1
		DRAUGHT:	9.0
		GROSS TONNAGE:	540.6

BUILT: 1849 - New York, New York.

HISTORY: Used at New York, 1888-1894.

STATUS: Burned at Port Richmond, Staten Island, New York, 1894.

CITY OF NEWPORT

ROUTE: Providence - Newport
PORTS: Providence, Newport
COMPANY: Continental Steamboat Co.

NUMBER: 5033
LENGTH: 177.5
BREADTH: 28.5
DRAUGHT: 8.8
GROSS TONNAGE: 561.0

BUILT: 1863 - New York, New York.
STATUS: Stranded and broken up on Prudence Island, Rhode Island, 1916.

PERRY

ROUTE: Narragansett Bay
PORTS: Providence, Newport
COMPANY: American Steamboat Co.
OTHER NAME: *DELAWARE*

NUMBER: 19919
LENGTH: 151.0
BREADTH: 24.7
DRAUGHT: 7.0
GROSS TONNAGE: 382.1

BUILT: 1845 - Brooklyn, New York
HISTORY: Narragansett Bay service until used during Civil War by United States Government. Delaware River service after the War.
STATUS: Burned at Wilmington, Delaware, May 20, 1896.

EOLUS

ROUTE: Wickford - Newport
PORTS: Wickford, Newport
COMPANY: Newport & Wickford
              Newport, Wickford Railroad & Steamboat Co.
OTHER NAME   *ISABEL*
BUILT: 1864 - Newburgh, New York.
HISTORY: Ran at Baltimore first. Went to Narragansett Bay, 1869.
STATUS: Dismantled, 1894.

NUMBER: 7814
LENGTH: 144.0
BREADTH: 25.0
DRAUGHT: 10.2
GROSS TONNAGE: 371.2

Steamship Historical Society of America, Inc.

WHAT CHEER

ROUTE:	Providence River	NUMBER:	26884
PORTS:	Providence, Fall River	LENGTH:	117.0
COMPANY:	Providence, Fall River, Newport	BREADTH:	23.0
	Steamboat Co.	DRAUGHT:	7.0
LOCATION:	Providence, Rhode Island	GROSS TONNAGE:	214.0
BUILT:	1867 - Keyport, New Jersey.		
HISTORY:	In New York, 1916-1920.		
STATUS:	Broken up about 1922 at New Rochelle, New York.		

WARWICK

ROUTE:	Narragansett Bay	NUMBER:	678
PORTS:	Providence, Fall River	LENGTH:	193.0
COMPANY:	Providence, Fall River & Newport	BREADTH:	30.5
	Steamboat Co.	DRAUGHT:	10.1
OTHER NAME:	*DAY STAR*	GROSS TONNAGE:	681.0
LOCATION:	Providence, Rhode Island		
BUILT:	1873 - Greenpoint, New York.		
STATUS:	Broken up at Staten Island, New York, 1935.		

HERMAN S. CASWELL

ROUTE: Newport - Narragansett Pier
PORTS: Newport, Narragansett Pier
COMPANY: Wm. C. Caswell
OTHER NAMES: *H. S. CASWELL, MARILDA II*

BUILT: 1878 - Noank, Connecticut.
HISTORY: Owned by Goodwin Steamship Corporation, 1926.
                Owned by Manhattan Yacht Cruises, Inc., 1939.
                Renamed *MARILDA II*, January, 1939.

NUMBER: 95530
LENGTH: 82.8
BREADTH: 17.7
DRAUGHT: 7.3
GROSS TONNAGE: 114.07

BALTIMORE

ROUTE:	Excursion Trade on Narragansett Bay	NUMBER:	3194
PORTS:	Providence, Newport	LENGTH:	100.0
COMPANY:	Providence, Fall River & Newport	BREADTH:	22.0
	Steamboat Co.	DRAUGHT:	6.8
OTHER NAME:	*POMHAM*	GROSS TONNAGE:	161.0
LOCATION:	Narragansett Bay		
BUILT:	1881 - Athens, New York.		
STATUS:	Abandoned, June 30, 1931.		

ISLANDER

ROUTE: Providence - Little Compton (Sakonnet)
PORTS: Providence, Little Compton, Rhode Island
COMPANY: Seaconnet Steamboat Co.

NUMBER: 100328
LENGTH: 106.2
BREADTH: 19.0
DRAUGHT: 6.8
GROSS TONNAGE: 119.0

BUILT: 1883 - Bath, Maine.
HISTORY: Service on the Kennebec River, Maine, first.
Service in New York City.
STATUS: Burned June 2, 1926, at Southport, North Carolina.

CITY OF PAWTUCKET

ROUTE: Providence River

BUILT: 1885 - Athens, New York.
STATUS: Sold to Venezuela, 1886.

NUMBER: 126300
LENGTH: 72.3
BREADTH: 9.7
DRAUGHT: 5.4
GROSS TONNAGE: 64.7

MOUNT HOPE

ROUTE: The Narragansett Bay Service   NUMBER: 92002
COMPANY: Newport, Wickford, Railroad & Steamboat Co.   LENGTH: 193.1
                                                                      BREADTH: 58.8
                                                                      DRAUGHT: 11.5
                                                                      GROSS TONNAGE: 880.0

BUILT: 1888 - Chelsea, Massachusetts.
HISTORY: Providence - Newport - Block Island route, forty-seven years.
STATUS: Dismantled, Providence, Rhode Island, 1936.

TOCKWOGH

ROUTE:	Wickford Line	NUMBER:	145523
PORTS:	Newport, Wickford	LENGTH:	166.0
COMPANY:	Newport, Wickford, Railroad & Steamboat Co.	BREADTH:	30.0
		DRAUGHT:	8.6
		GROSS TONNAGE:	457.3
BUILT:	1889 - Baltimore, Maryland.		
STATUS:	Burned at Wickford Landing, April 11, 1893.		

GENERAL

ROUTE:	Wickford - Newport	NUMBER:	86056
PORTS:	Wickford, Newport	LENGTH:	130.0
COMPANY:	New England Steamship Co.	BREADTH:	25.1
		DRAUGHT:	9.4
		GROSS TONNAGE:	332.0

BUILT: 1889 - Brooklyn, New York.

HISTORY: Wickford - Newport, 1893-1925.
             New York Harbor, Battery to Statue of Liberty later.

STATUS: Broken up, November, 1935, foot of First St. Bridge, Elizabeth, New Jersey.

MUNNATAWKET

ROUTE:	Narragansett Bay	NUMBER:	92197
		LENGTH:	117.0
		BREADTH:	22.4
		DRAUGHT:	8.5
		GROSS TONNAGE:	204.6

BUILT: 1890 - New London, Connecticut.
HISTORY: 1905 Boston to Nahant Run.
1909-1911 Portsmouth to Isles of Shoals Run.
1920-1931 Fisher's Island Run.
STATUS: Destroyed by fire, September 11, 1935, at Hicks Wharf, Norfolk, Virginia.

AWASHONKS

ROUTE: Providence - Seaconnet, also
Excursion Service in Narragansett Bay
PORTS: Providence, Bristol, Seaconnet
COMPANY: Seaconnet Steamboat Co.

NUMBER: 107011
LENGTH: 107.4
BREADTH: 17.0
DRAUGHT: 7.0
GROSS TONNAGE: 165.5

BUILT: 1893 - Barbour Brothers, Brewer, Maine.
STATUS: Destroyed by fire off Tiverton, Rhode Island, April 21, 1901.

BAY QUEEN

ROUTE: Narragansett Bay
PORTS: Providence, Newport
COMPANY: American Steamboat Co.
OTHER NAMES: *HINGHAM, ORIENT*

BUILT: 1865 - Brooklyn, New York.
HISTORY: Narragansett Bay Service entire life.
STATUS: Dismantled in Providence, Rhode Island, May 5, 1906.

NUMBER: 2410
LENGTH: 184.3
BREADTH: 29.6
DRAUGHT: 9.6
GROSS TONNAGE: 679.5

NEW SHOREHAM

ROUTE:	Providence - Block Island	NUMBER:	130934
PORTS:	Providence, Block Island	LENGTH:	151.9
COMPANY:	Town of New Shoreham	BREADTH:	28.1
OTHER NAMES:	*MYRTLE II, PRISCILLA ALDEN*	DRAUGHT:	11.8
		GROSS TONNAGE:	503.0

BUILT: 1901 - William McKie, Boston, Massachusetts.

HISTORY: Ran Block Island Line, 1901-1929.
Excursion service, Boston Harbor, 1935.
Boston to Plymouth, Massachusetts, 1935.
Bridgeport to Port Jefferson, 1940.

STATUS: Dismantled, 1955.

Steamship Historical Society of America, Inc.

MONHEGAN

ROUTE:	Narragansett Bay	NUMBER:	93395
PORTS:	Providence, Newport	LENGTH:	128.0
COMPANY:	Providence, Fall River & Newport	BREADTH:	26.7
	Steamboat Co.	DRAUGHT:	11.2
LOCATION:	Narragansett Bay	GROSS TONNAGE:	387.0
BUILT:	1903 - Cobb-Butler Yard, Rockland, Maine.		
HISTORY:	Operated between Portland and Rockland first part of life, together with *MINEOLA* in Eastern Steamship Company's service.		
STATUS:	Wrecked during 1938 hurricane at Providence, Rhode Island.		

See page 80

Steamship Historical Society of America, Inc.

MAY ARCHER

ROUTE:	Narragansett Bay	NUMBER:	203190
PORTS:	Providence, Newport	LENGTH:	80.3
COMPANY:	Rhode Island Marine Transportation Co.	BREADTH:	20.0
LOCATION:	Providence, Rhode Island, Harbor	DRAUGHT:	7.8
		GROSS TONNAGE:	125.0

BUILT: 1906 - Cobb-Butler Yard, Rockland, Maine.
HISTORY: Boothbay, Thomaston, Monhegan Island, Maine, early part of her life.
STATUS: Total loss by fire, May 30, 1934, Quincy, Massachusetts.

See page 160

FAVORITE

ROUTE:	Providence - Seaconnet Point, Rhode Island	NUMBER:		120967
PORTS:	Providence, Bristol, Seaconnet	LENGTH:		127.6
COMPANY:	Seaconnet Steamboat Co.	BREADTH:		30.6
		DRAUGHT:		8.2
		GROSS TONNAGE:		399.0
BUILT:	1894 - Tompkins Grove, New York.			
HISTORY:	Sailed out of Providence, Rhode Island, 1902.			
STATUS:	Abandoned, 1940.			

MACKINAC

ROUTE:	Narragansett Bay	NUMBER:	206658
PORTS:	Providence, Narragansett Bay Ports	LENGTH:	162.0
COMPANY:	Mackinac Co. of Rhode Island	BREADTH:	28.2
OTHER NAME:	*WOONSOCKET*	DRAUGHT:	12.0
		GROSS TONNAGE:	512.0

BUILT: 1909 - Ferrysburg, Michigan.

HISTORY: Boiler exploded, August 18, 1925, in Narragansett Bay, thirty-five fatalities. Renamed *WOONSOCKET*, July 9, 1926, Motorized, 1937. Norfolk, Baltimore & Carolina Lines, Inc., 1968.

Chapter 20

Block Island Vessels

Steamers servicing this island maintained more prominence than in many other areas of New England, since competition from other means of transportation for permanent and summer residents did not exist..

The famous Captain Raymond H. Abell, who operated the Interstate Navigation Company, played an important part in developing the Block Island Steamship services. Several ships under his management are shown in this chapter with Block Island steamers: *G. W. DANIELSON, BLOCK ISLAND WESTPORT, CHAUNCEY M. DEPEW, NELSECO II, ELIZABETH ANN, SPRIGG CARROLL, PEMAQUID, YANKEE, BLOCK ISLAND* (2), *SAGAMORE, CAMBRIDGE, NAUGATUCK* and *BLOCK ISLAND* (3).

Captain Raymond H. Abell

G. W. DANIELSON

ROUTE: Providence - Block Island
PORTS: Providence, Block Island
OTHER NAMES: *AMERICANA, BARTON BROTHERS,*
               AMBROSE IV

NUMBER: 85618
LENGTH: 106.5
BREADTH: 21.6
DRAUGHT: 8.5
GROSS TONNAGE: 130.7

BUILT: 1880 - Mystic Bridge, Connecticut.
HISTORY: Renamed *AMERICANA*, 1914. 1918, New York Steam Lighter. 1924, renamed *AMBROSE IV*.
STATUS: Dismantled, September, 1938, New York, New York.

Steamship Historical Society of America, Inc.

BLOCK ISLAND (2)

ROUTE:	Block Island Line	NUMBER:	203969
PORTS:	Providence, Block Island	LENGTH:	136.5
COMPANY:	Interstate Navigation Co.	BREADTH:	29.0
OTHER NAMES:	*MACHIGONNE, HOOK MT.,*	DRAUGHT:	9.6
	LEAGUE ISLAND, YANKEE	GROSS TONNAGE:	425.0
BUILT:	1907 - Neafie & Levy, Philadelphia, Pennsylvania.		
HISTORY:	Started service on Casco Bay Lines running from Portland to various ports in Casco Bay. See Page 209 *MACHIGONNE*, page 399 *YANKEE*.		

WESTPORT

ROUTE:	Providence - Block Island	NUMBER:	208731
PORTS:	Providence, Newport, Block Island	LENGTH:	125.6
COMPANY:	Interstate Navigation Co.	BREADTH:	21.2
OTHER NAMES:	*COLONEL LOUIS F. GERRARD,*	DRAUGHT:	8.8
SISTER SHIP:	*SOUTHPORT*	GROSS TONNAGE:	188.0
LOCATION:	On the Providence - Block Island Line		

BUILT: 1911 - William McKie, East Boston, Massachusetts.

HISTORY: Built for Eastern Steamship Lines for service between Bath and Boothbay. Later ran from Rockland to Blue Hill, also to Bar Harbor. Controlled by United States Army during World War I. 1937-1939, ran Providence to Block Island. 1940, ran Norwich, New London, to Block Island. 1941, purchased by United States Maritime Commission for use during World War II.

STATUS: Abandoned, Newark, New Jersey, 1958.

CHAUNCEY M. DEPEW

ROUTE:	Providence - Newport - Block Island	NUMBER:	211290
PORTS:	Providence, Newport, Block Island	LENGTH:	185.1
COMPANY:	Interstate Navigation Co.	BREADTH:	35.6
OTHER NAME:	*RANGELEY*	DRAUGHT:	13.5
SISTER SHIP:	*MOOSEHEAD*	GROSS TONNAGE:	652.0
LOCATION:	On the Providence - Block Island Line.		
BUILT:	1913 - Bath Iron Works, Inc., Bath, Maine.		
HISTORY:	Built for the Maine Central Railroad, operated on Line to Mount Desert Island, 1913-1925. Ran Hudson River Day Line, 1926. Requisitioned during World War II by United States Government. Boston - Princetown. Boston - Block Island. New York City - Atlantic Island. Hamilton, Bermuda, as Tender, 1968.		
STATUS:	Hackensack River, 1977.		

Mariners Museum, Newport News, Virginia

NELSECO II

ROUTE: New London - Block Island
PORTS: New London, Block Island
COMPANY: Interstate Navigation Co.
OTHER NAMES: *COLONEL JOSEPH F. TAUIBEE,*

BUILT: 1917 - Boothbay Harbor, Maine.
HISTORY: Ran for United States Government, World War II.
STATUS: Running, 1968.

NUMBER: 215592
LENGTH: 110.5
BREADTH: 29.0
DRAUGHT: 8.2
GROSS TONNAGE: 237.0

Captain Raymond H. Abel

ELIZABETH ANN

ROUTE: Block Island Line
PORTS: New London, Block Island
COMPANY: Interstate Navigation Co.
OTHER NAME: *USN SUBMARINE CHASER #127*
SISTER SHIPS: Submarine chasers in World War I
BUILT: 1917 - Norfolk Navy Yard, Norfolk, Virginia.
STATUS: Burned, New London, Connecticut, April 1, 1951.

NUMBER: 222509
LENGTH: 104.3
BREADTH: 14.6
DRAUGHT: 7.9
GROSS TONNAGE: 77.0

SPRIGG CARROLL

ROUTE:	New London - Block Island	NUMBER:	251310
PORTS:	New London, Block Island	LENGTH:	100.0
COMPANY:	Interstate Navigation Co.	BREADTH:	24.0
OTHER NAME:	*U.S.S. SPRIGG CARROLL*	DRAUGHT:	11.8
LOCATION:	On the New London - Block Island Line	GROSS TONNAGE:	282.0

BUILT: 1903 - Pusey & Jones Co., Wilmington, Delaware.

HISTORY: Built for Quartermaster Corps, United States Army. Used in Portland and Casco Bay, Maine. Nelseco Navigation Co., New London, Connecticut, 1947.

STATUS: Running, 1968.

PEMAQUID

ROUTE: Block Island Line
PORTS: New London, Block Island
COMPANY: Sound Steamship Lines, Inc.
OTHER NAMES: *LONG ISLAND,*
U.S.S. MAJOR JACOB ALONZO HOWE
BUILT: 1893 - Neafie & Levy, Philadelphia, Pennsylvania.
HISTORY: Ran for Maine Central Railroad in Maine, July, 1901, until June 25, 1931. On Statue of Liberty Run, New York City, 1950.
STATUS: Owned by Edward Pajus, Jr., New York City, 1968. Running, 1979.

NUMBER: 141270
LENGTH: 132.5
BREADTH: 28.0
DRAUGHT: 9.8
GROSS TONNAGE: 420.0

Captain Raymond H. Abell

YANKEE

ROUTE:	Block Island Line	NUMBER:	203969
PORTS:	New London, Block Island	LENGTH:	136.5
OTHER NAMES:	*MACHIGONNE, HOOK MT.,*	BREADTH:	29.0
	LEAGUE ISLAND, BLOCK ISLAND (2)	DRAUGHT:	9.6
		GROSS TONNAGE:	425.0

BUILT: 1907 - Neafie & Levy, Philadelphia, Pennsylvania.

HISTORY: Bought as *M.V. HOOK MT.* in 1940. Ran for one year Providence, Newport, Block Island. Sold to United States Navy, 1941. Brought back to Philadelphia, 1946. Renamed *BLOCK ISLAND*. Ran one year, Providence, Newport, Block Island. Equipped with new 900 hp. engine, name changed to *YANKEE*, 1947.

STATUS: Running, 1979.

BLOCK ISLAND

ROUTE:	New London - Block Island	NUMBER:		320
PORTS:	New London, Block Island	LENGTH:		187.
COMPANY:	New London Steamboat Co.	BREADTH:		32.
		DRAUGHT:		11
		GROSS TONNAGE:		757

BUILT: 1882 - Noank, Connecticut.

HISTORY: In 1901, the New York, New Haven, Hartford Railroad took over the financially disabled New Londe
Steamboat Co. Also the New England Steamship Co., which became the owner.

STATUS: Abandoned, June 30, 1926.

NOTE: Looking at the picture - "Where were the Coast Guard inspectors?"

SAGAMORE

ROUTE:	New London - Block Island	NUMBER:	116821
PORTS:	New London, Block Island	LENGTH:	82.4
COMPANY:	Rhode Island Marine Transportation Co.	BREADTH:	20.2
		DRAUGHT:	8.6
		GROSS TONNAGE:	104.0

BUILT: 1898 - New England Shipbuilding Co., Bath, Maine.
STATUS: Foundered three miles east of Brigantine Shoals, New Jersey, January 15, 1937.

CAMBRIDGE

ROUTE: New London - Block Island   NUMBER: 107216
PORTS: New London, Block Island   LENGTH: 225.3
COMPANY: Sound Steamship Lines, Inc.   BREADTH: 42.1
OTHER NAMES: *ATLANTA, MEXICAN,*   DRAUGHT: 14.0
    GROSS TONNAGE: 2094.0

BUILT: 1896 - Wm. Cramp & Sons, Philadelphia, Pennsylvania.

HISTORY: 1896-1914 Chesapeake Bay Service.
1915-1916 Gulf of Mexico.
1916-1938 New York - Providence Run.
1938-1941 Excursion boat New York and Long Island Sound.
1942 Philadelphia - Norfolk.
1943-1947 Amazon River with cargo booms added.

STATUS: Lost off coast of Brazil, May 1, 1950.

NAUGATUCK

ROUTE:	New London - Block Island	NUMBER:	127281
PORTS:	New London, Block Island	LENGTH:	220.7
COMPANY:	Sound Steamship Lines, Inc.	BREADTH:	37.2
OTHER NAMES:	*ALLAN JOY, CAPE CHARLES*	DRAUGHT:	14.0
		GROSS TONNAGE:	1164.0

BUILT:	1898 - Delaware River Shipbuilding Co., Chester, Pennsylvania.
HISTORY:	Purchased by Joy Line, 1899, renamed *ALLAN JOY*.
	Purchased by Bridgeport Steamboat Co., January 4, 1900.
	1924, cut down to a freight steamboat.
STATUS:	Dismantled, Baltimore, Maryland, 1956.

Wm. H. Ewen, Jr.

BLOCK ISLAND (3)

ROUTE: New London, Connecticut -
              Block Island, Rhode Island
PORTS: New London, Block Island
COMPANY: Nelseco Navigation Co.
OTHER NAMES: *FISHER'S ISLAND, U.S.S. COLONEL*
              JOHN E. BAXTER, FISHER'S ISLAND
BUILT: 1926 - Wilmington, Delaware.
HISTORY: Replaced *YANKEE* on New London - Block Island Service, August 3, 1961.

NUMBER: 226004
LENGTH: 150.0
BREADTH: 40.0
DRAUGHT: 14.4
GROSS TONNAGE: 862.0

INDEX